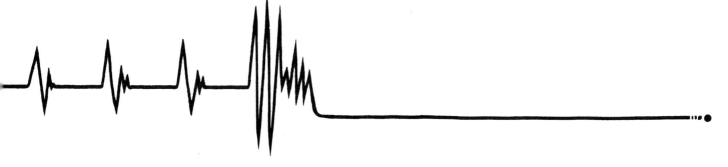

Unpleasant
Ways
To
Die.

Other books by elan:

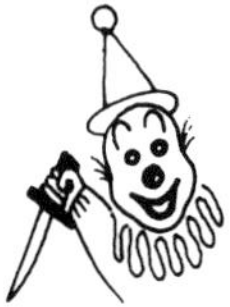

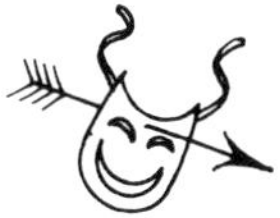

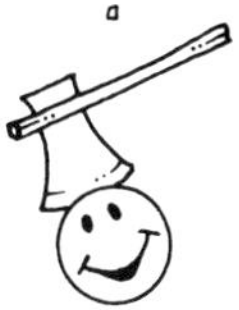

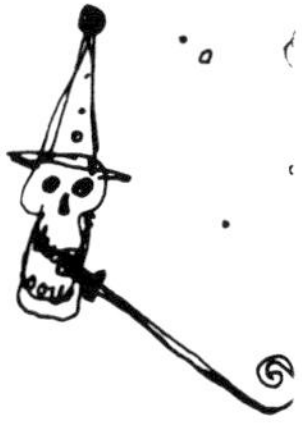

UNPLEASANT WAYS TO DIE

"humorous" drawings by elan fleisher

ST. MARTIN'S PRESS
NEW YORK CITY

For information, address ST. MARTIN'S PRESS, 175 Fifth Avenue, New York City, N.Y. 10010.

Library of Congress Cataloging-in-Publication Data

fleisher, elan

UNPLEASANT WAYS TO DIE

1. Death - Caricatures and Cartoons.
2. American Wit and Humor, Pictorial. I. Title.

NC1429. F614A4 1989 741.5'973 89-6267

ISBN 0-312-03269-2

FIRST EDITION 10 9 8 7 6 5 4

INSPIRATION NATION: Sucker MC's Fresh Def Jam Krush, Kold Krush Krew IN EFFECT, **Rick Rubin**, Satch + the Aztec Posse, Tompkins^2, **Brother Theodore,** Jam Master Jay (couldn't wait to see), **¡el diablo!,** West 31 St. Posse, SAVE THE ROBOTS, Supply Head, **Chuck D + Flav**, FRAMPTON!, Bud Puppet, **LL Kool Moe J,** the Mummenschänz Man, FROZEN EXPLOSION, **11 W. 10 St · 26**, Sid Vicious, Bill Buckner, **Tony Montana,** Dr. Winston O'Boogie, Africa Bambatta, **the Riceheads**, the swoopster, Big Daddy Kane + the Pop-O-Matic Posse, **Al Lewis**, Mitch Green, PAL 'N' ZUELA, Sammy Davis Sr., Sturgio, Simon + Simon Head, Al Goldstein, **King Ad Yauck + Mike Douche,** Gingster + the MARS^{10} Posse, Cybil Sheperd, **the Kiev**, Eric B + Rakim, **DMC** + the Hollis Populous, **WALLOWITCH**, Rasputin, A Candy Colored Clown they call the Sandman, **GrandMaster Flash,** Raye Hollitt, Sylvain^2, **UJ**, Rene Goulet, **MOE**, Kim Alexis, Tone-Lōc, Herve Villechaise, **Howard Stern**, Soup D Jour, MC Delite, **Dr. No**, Abdul O'toole, Star-Keen Nurd, **ICE T**, Doc Hoch + the Biscayne Posse, Carol Alt, **Bayamo's** Carrot Cake Surprise!, SHOCK D DAY, COLLIE MA, Old Blind Lemon, **the GATORS,** **DEF JAM**, Lincoln Hawk, Deborah Harry, Jello Biafra, MUSTANG 65, **R.K.** (He brives a dus), Chris Elliot, **Prof. Griff,** Joe Mannix, **Ax, Smash,** LumpHead, SprinklerHead, CascadeHead, PlummetHead, Sealy Poster Pedic Head, Night of the Living Dead Head, Weight of the World Head, Aint to Provd

Dedicated to
those of us who
will have
the pleasure

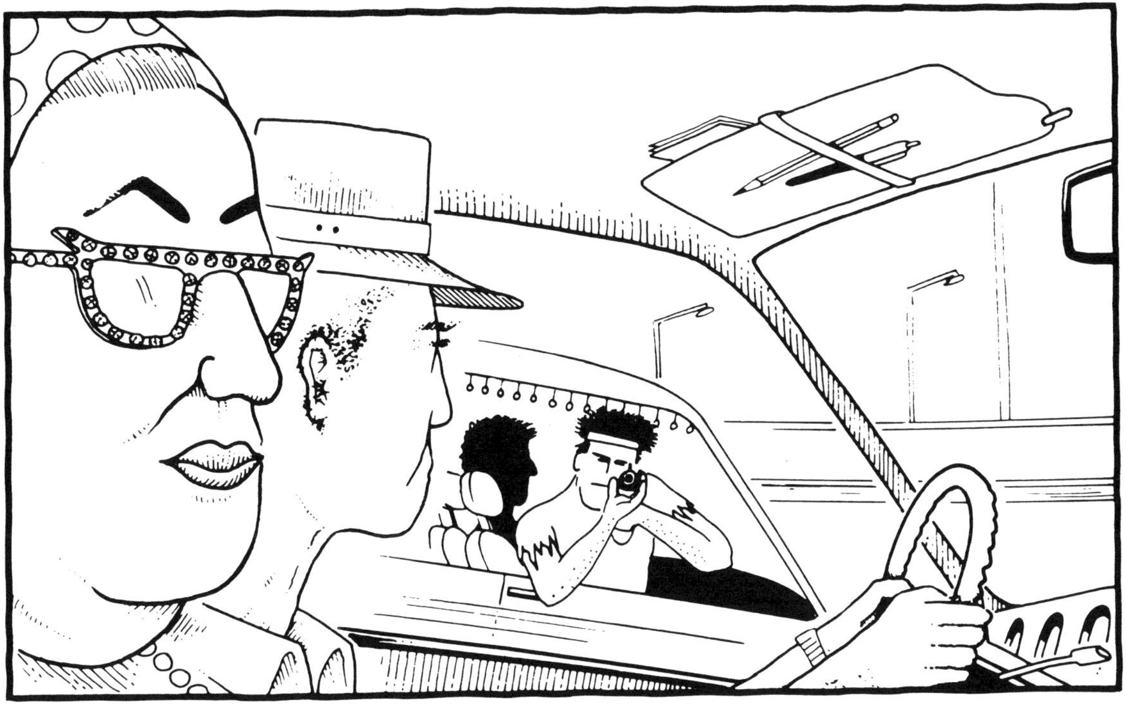

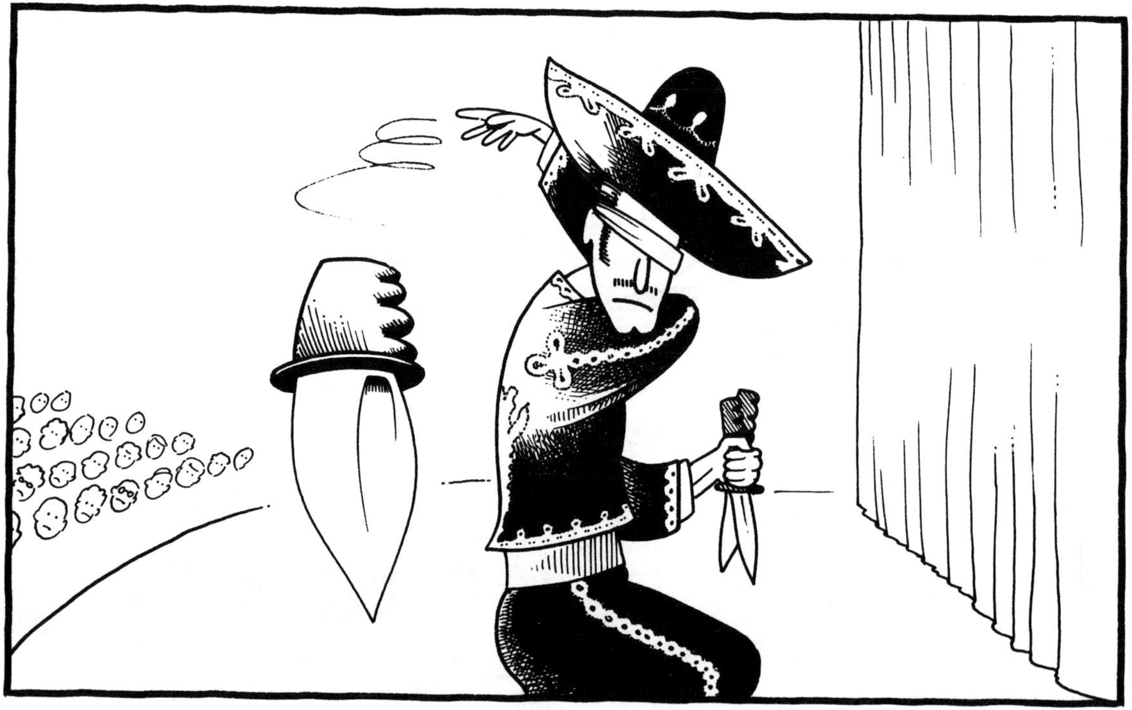

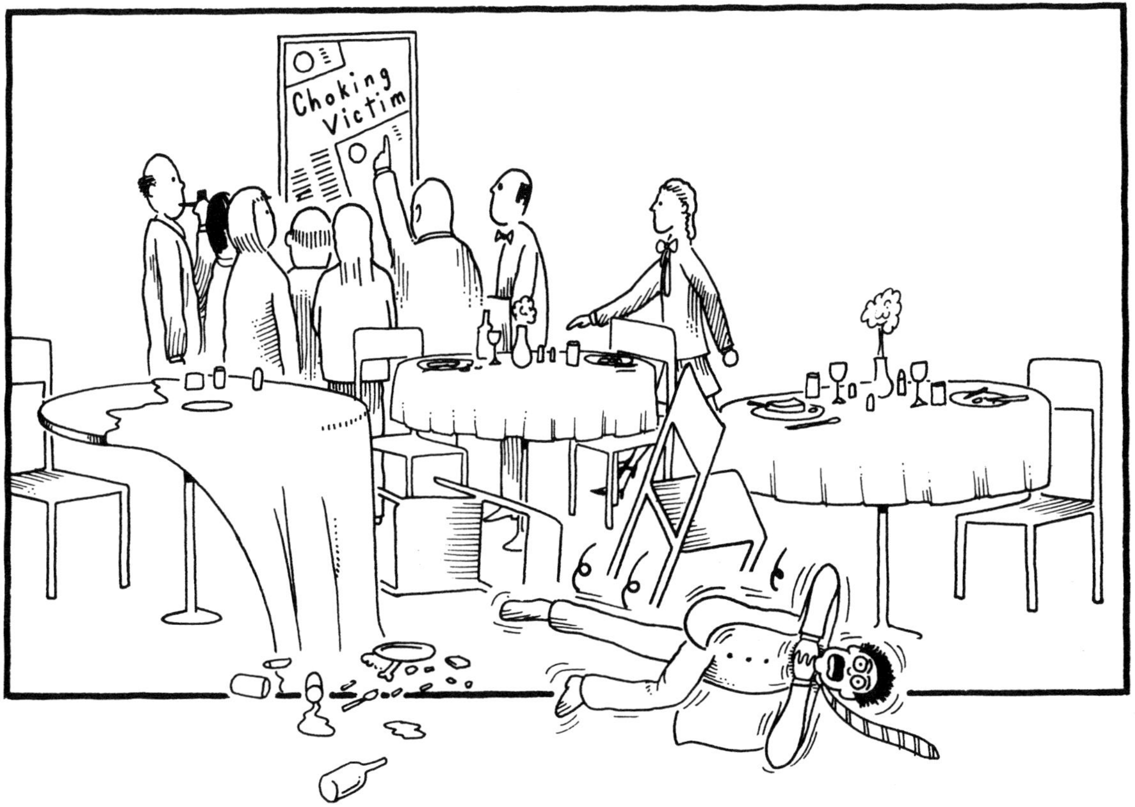
Choking Victim

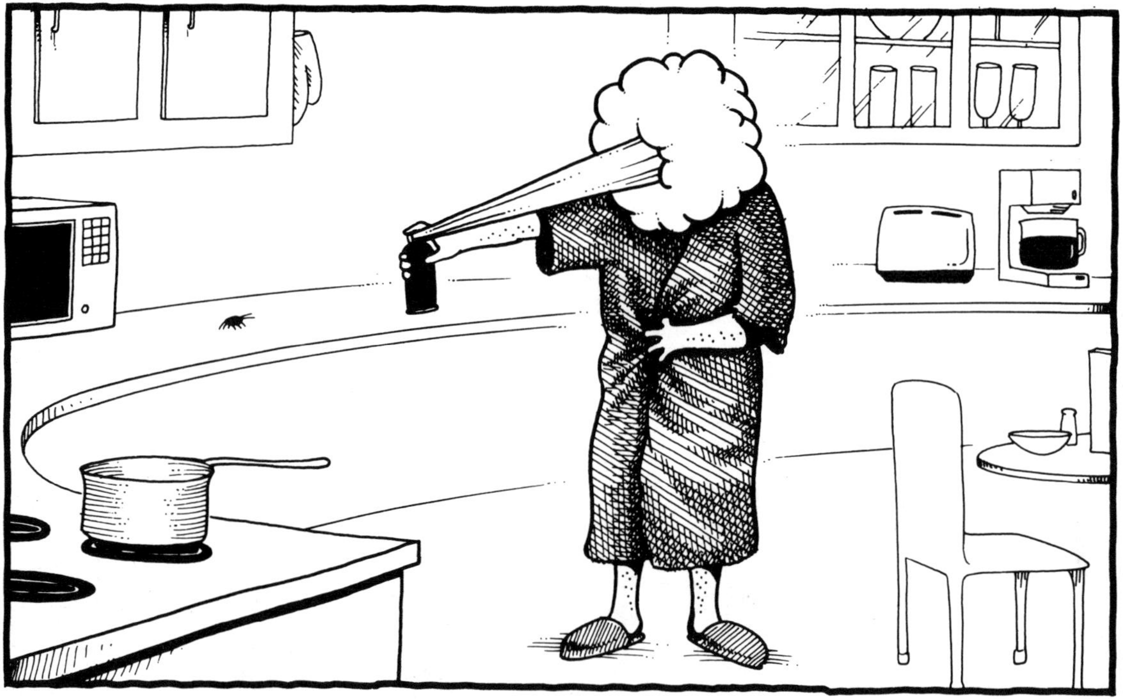

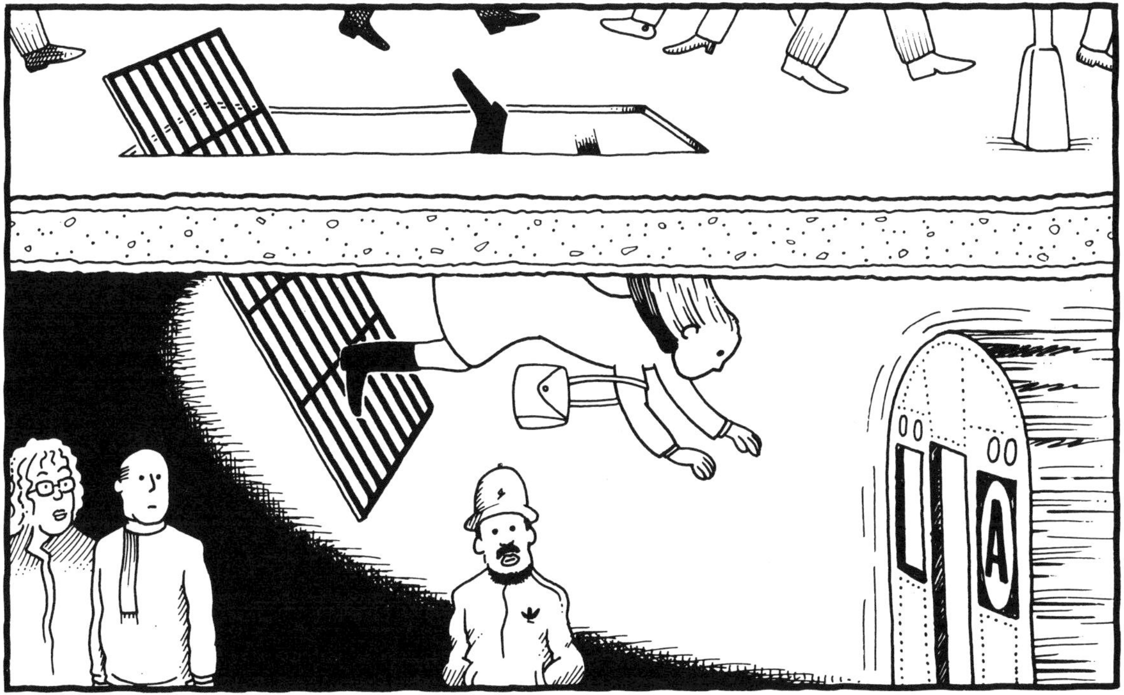
A

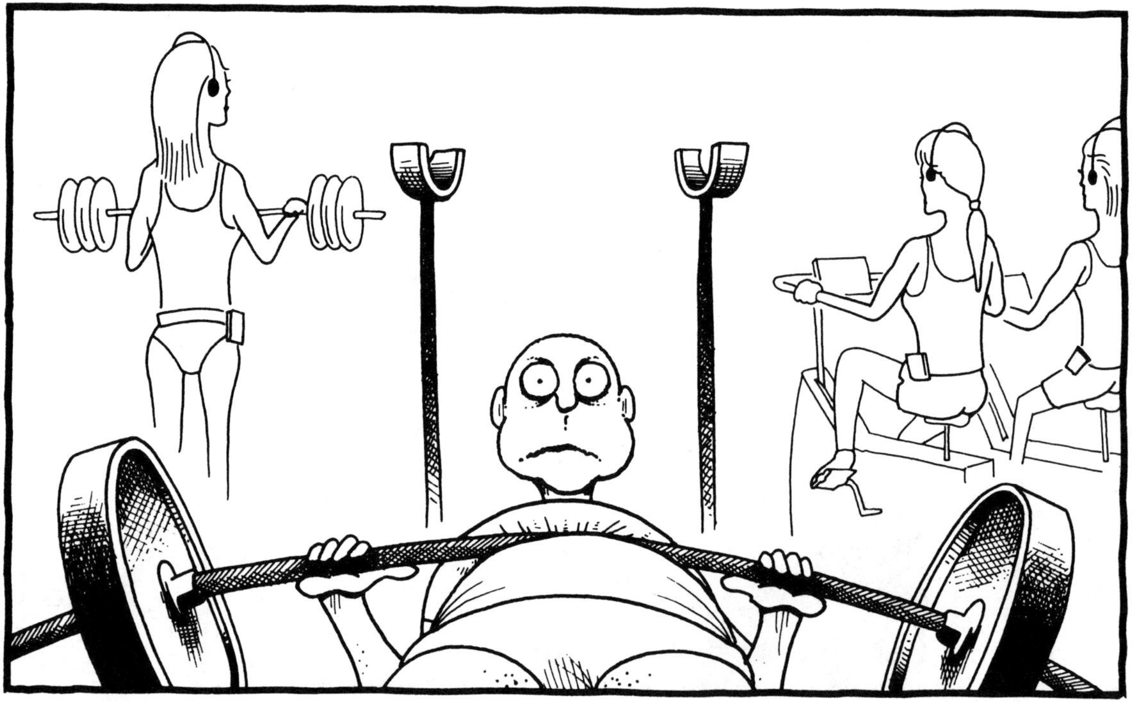

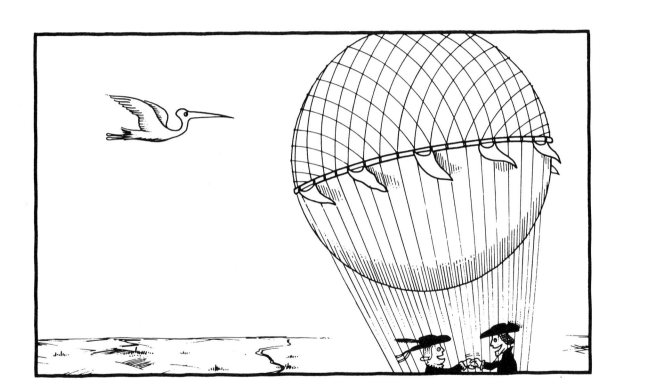

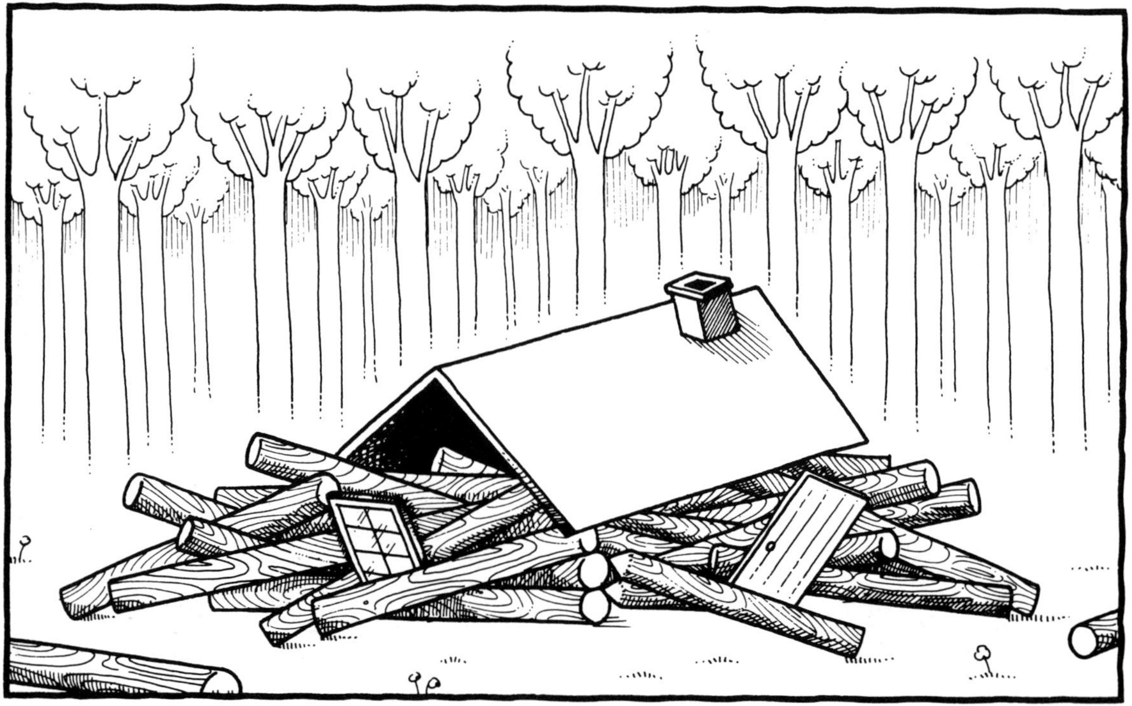

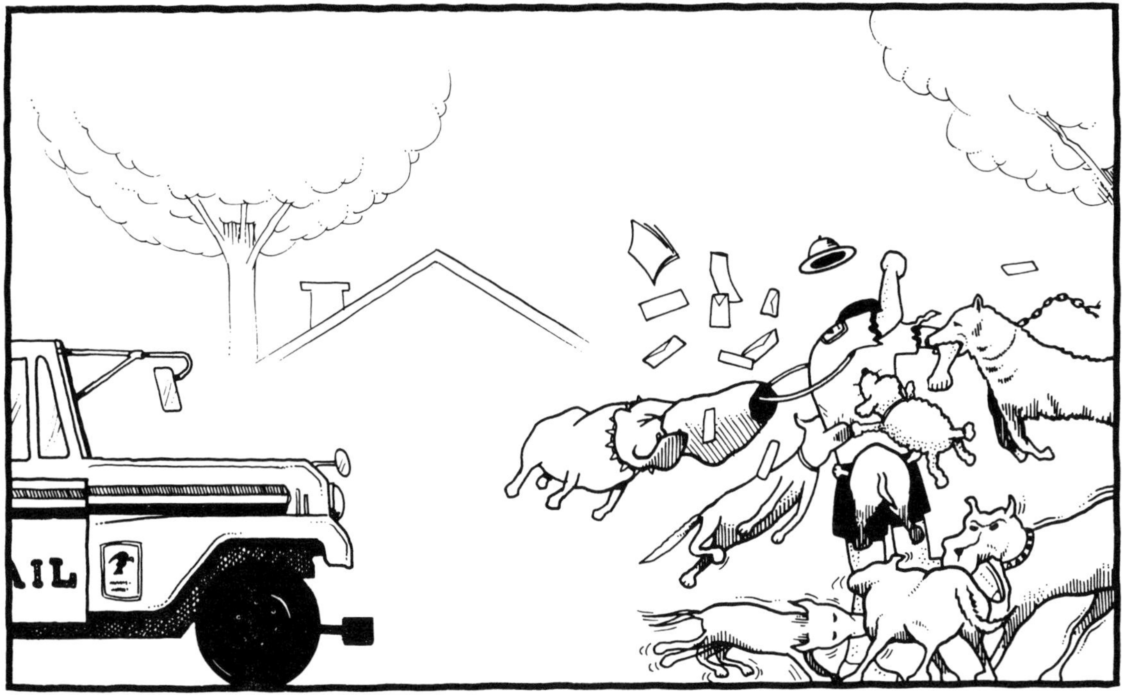
AIL

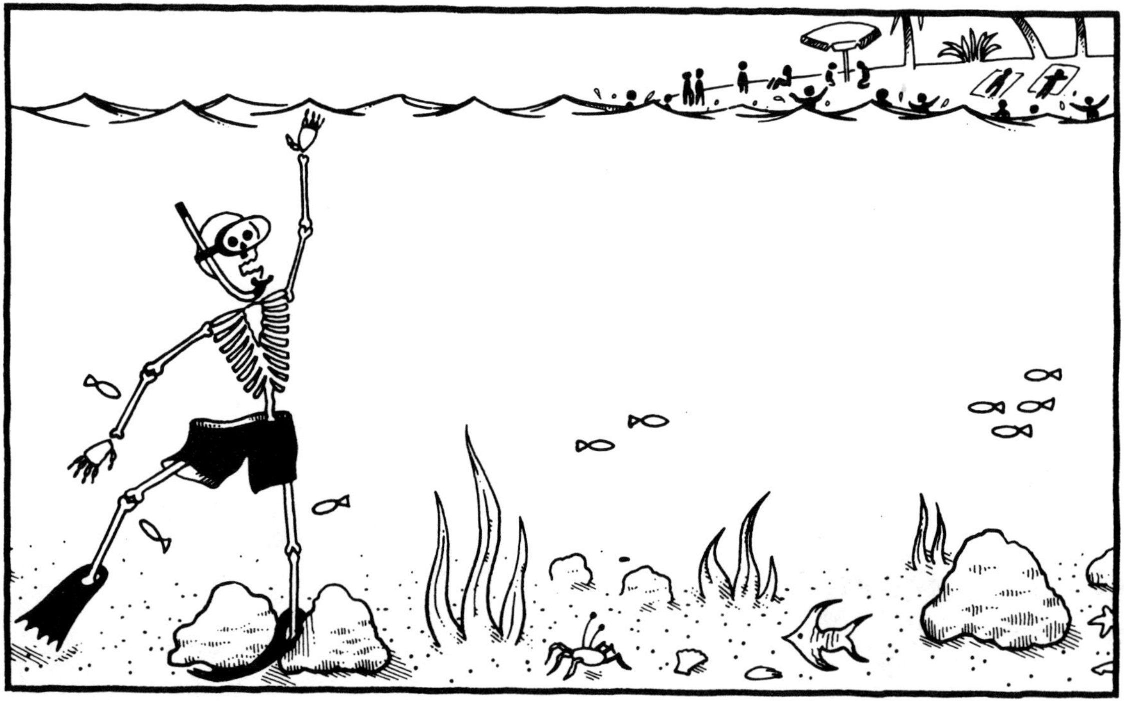

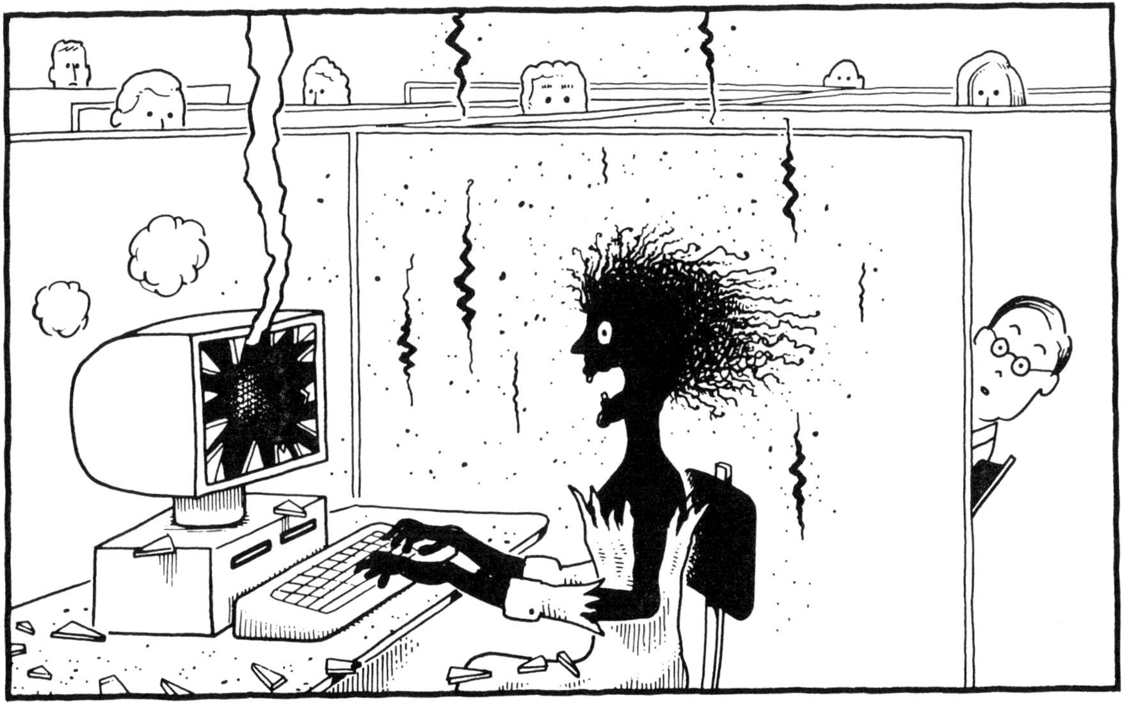

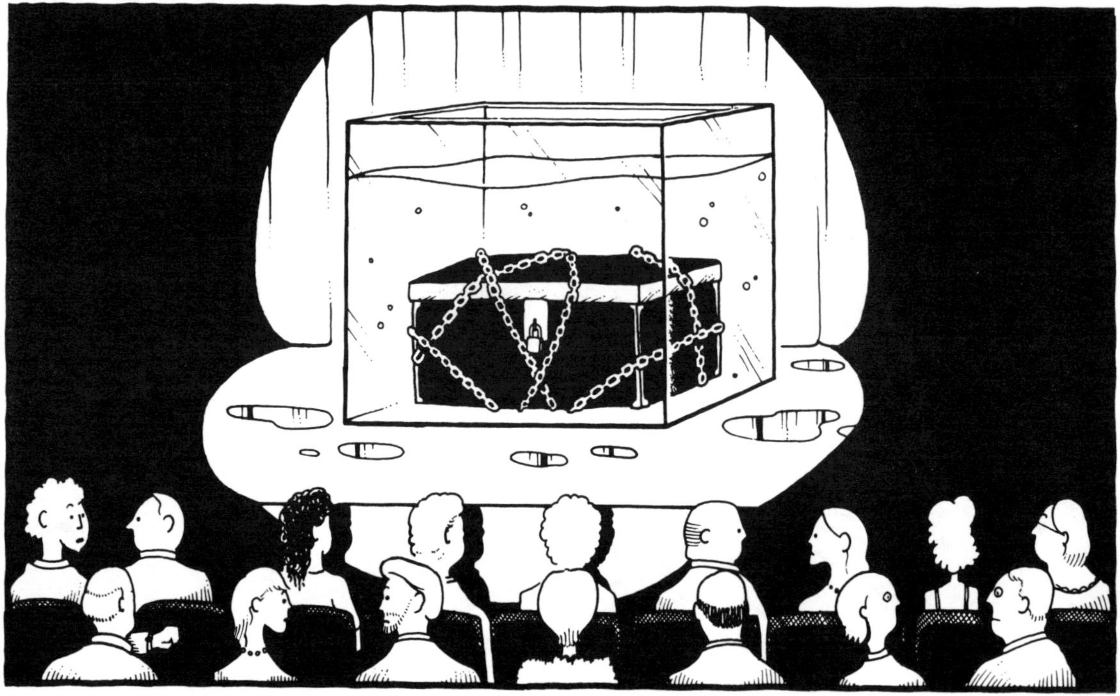

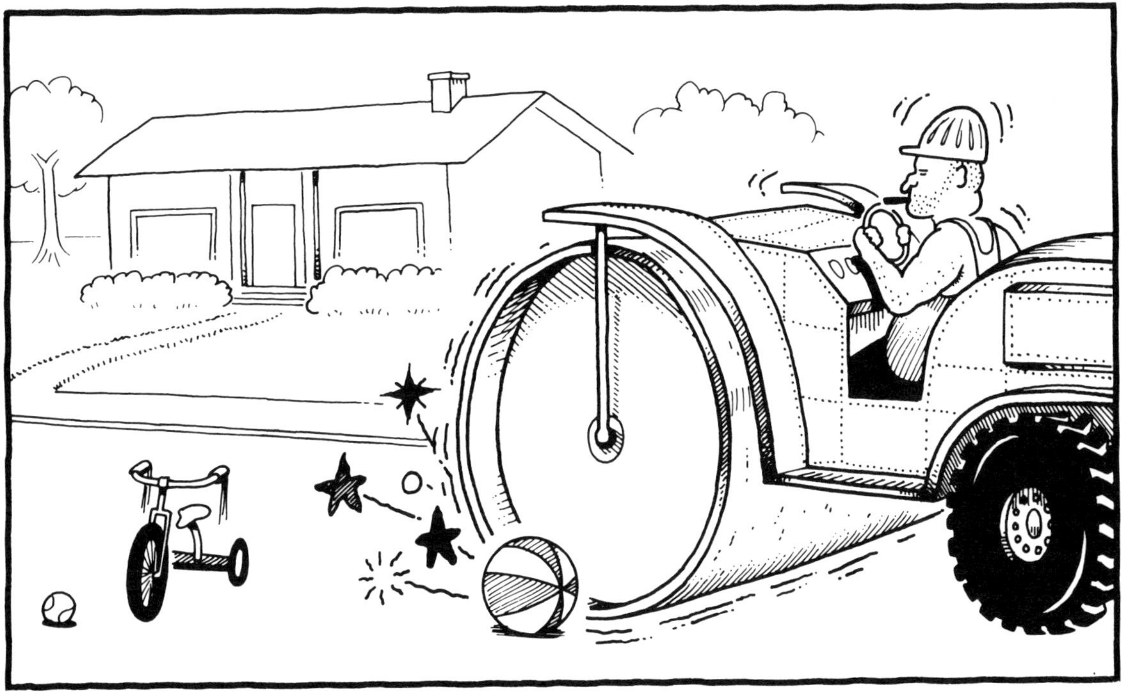

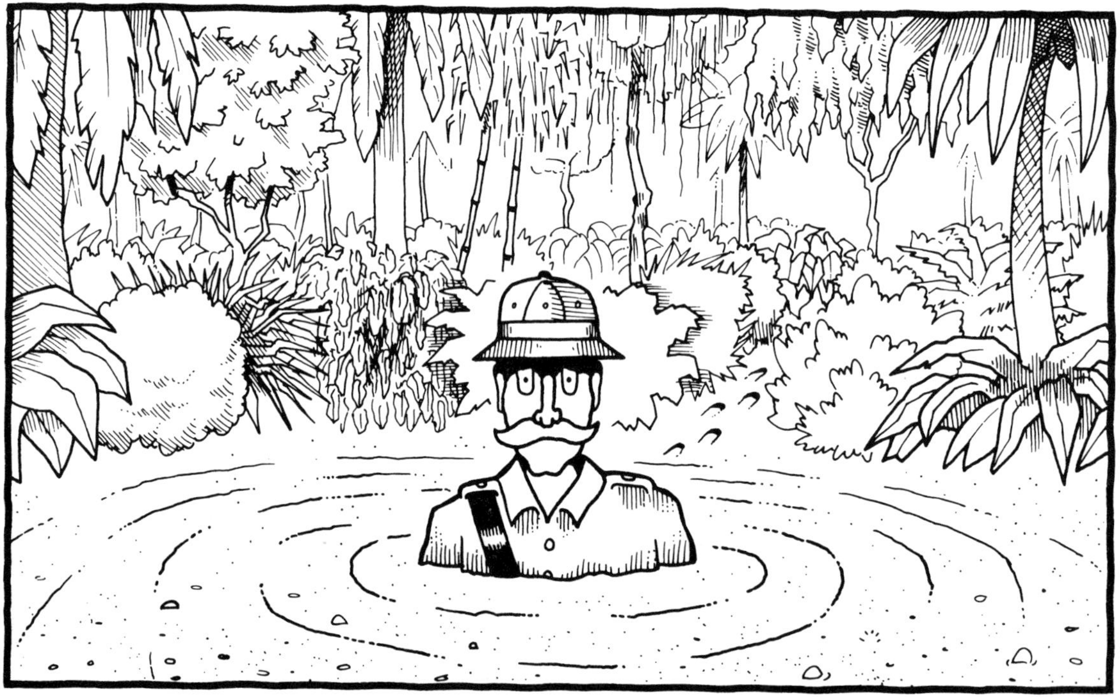

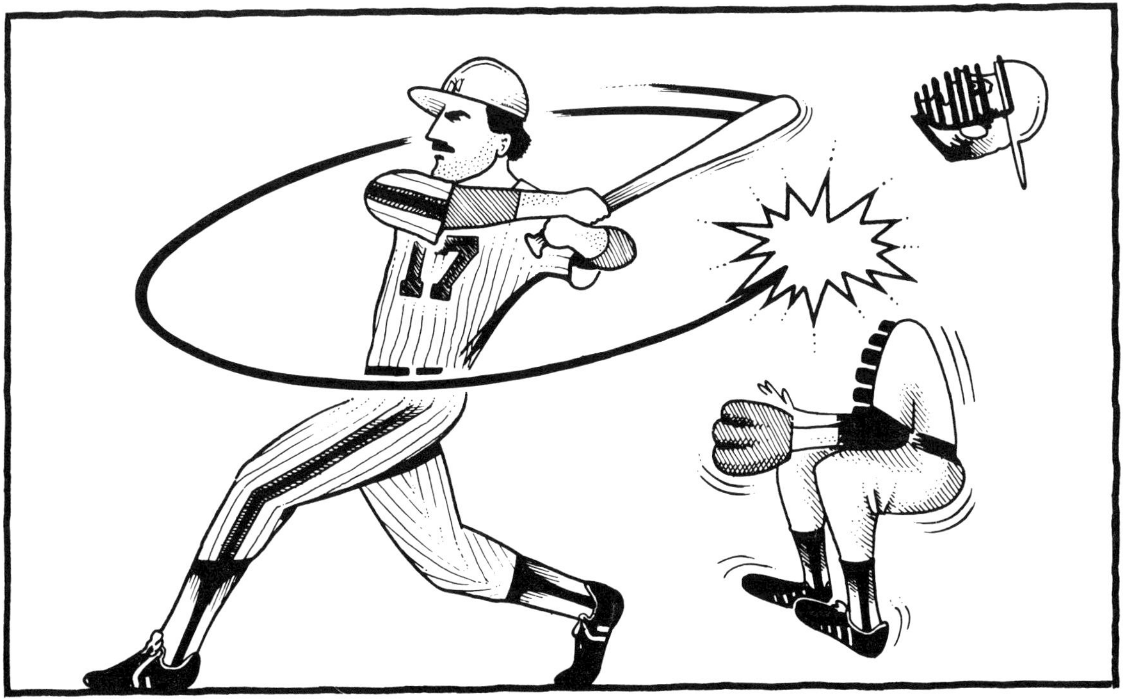

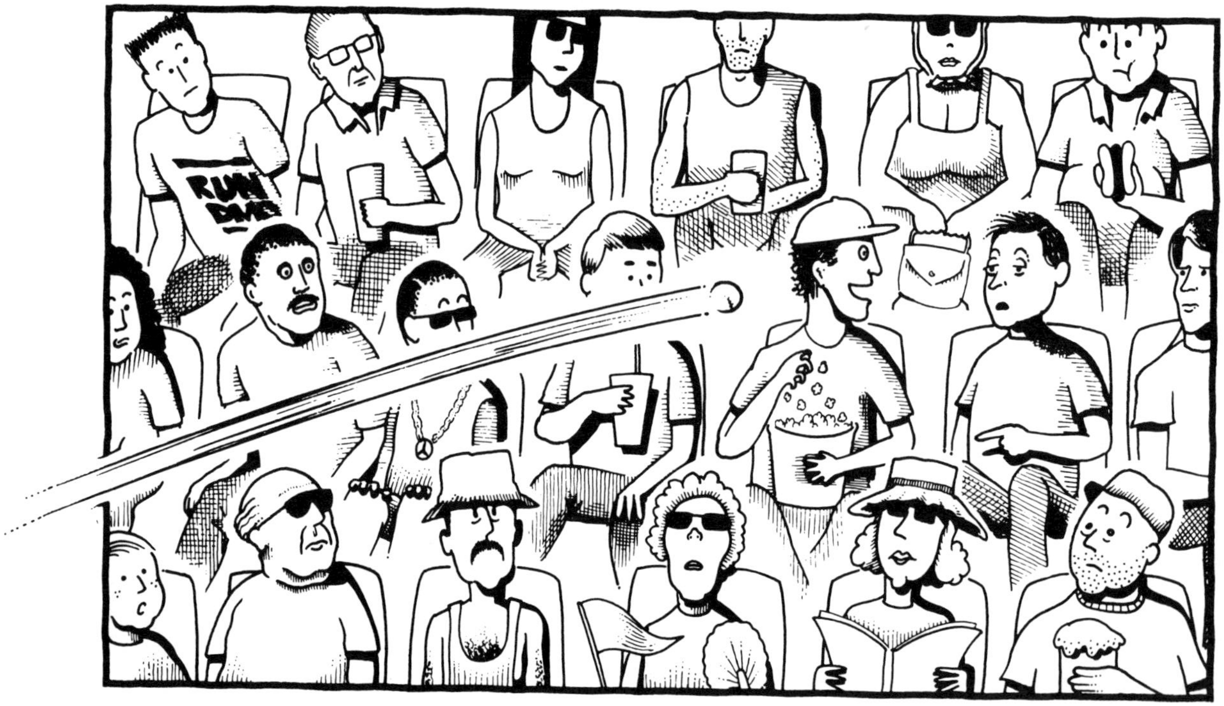
RUN DMC

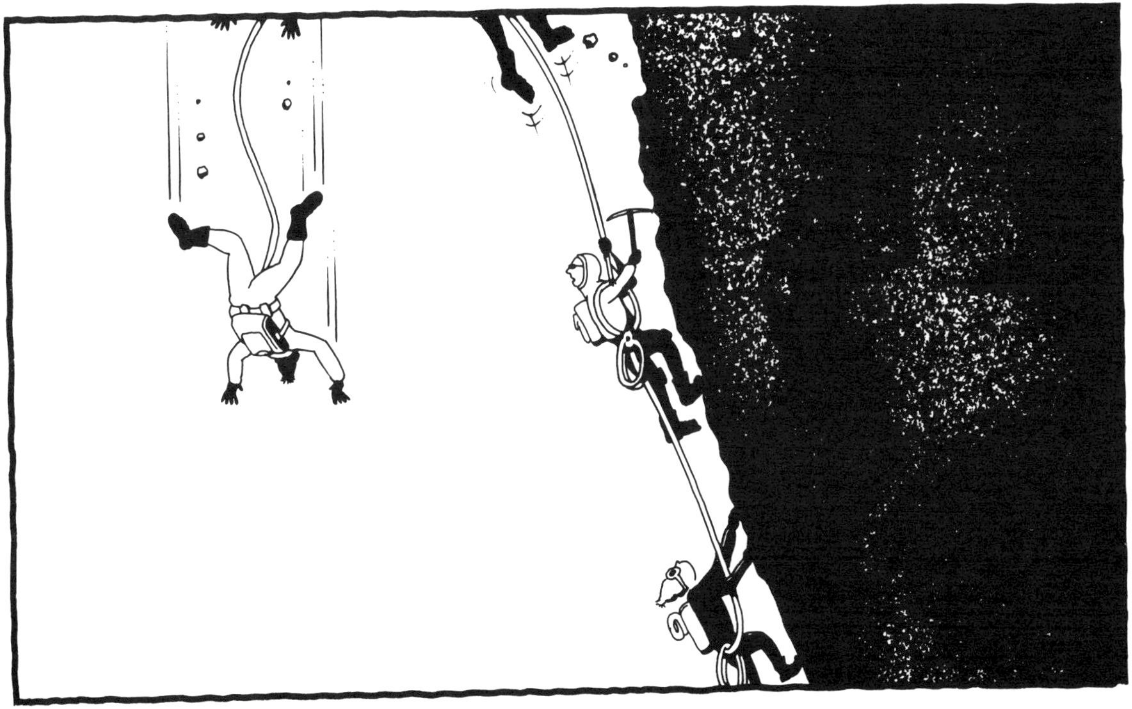

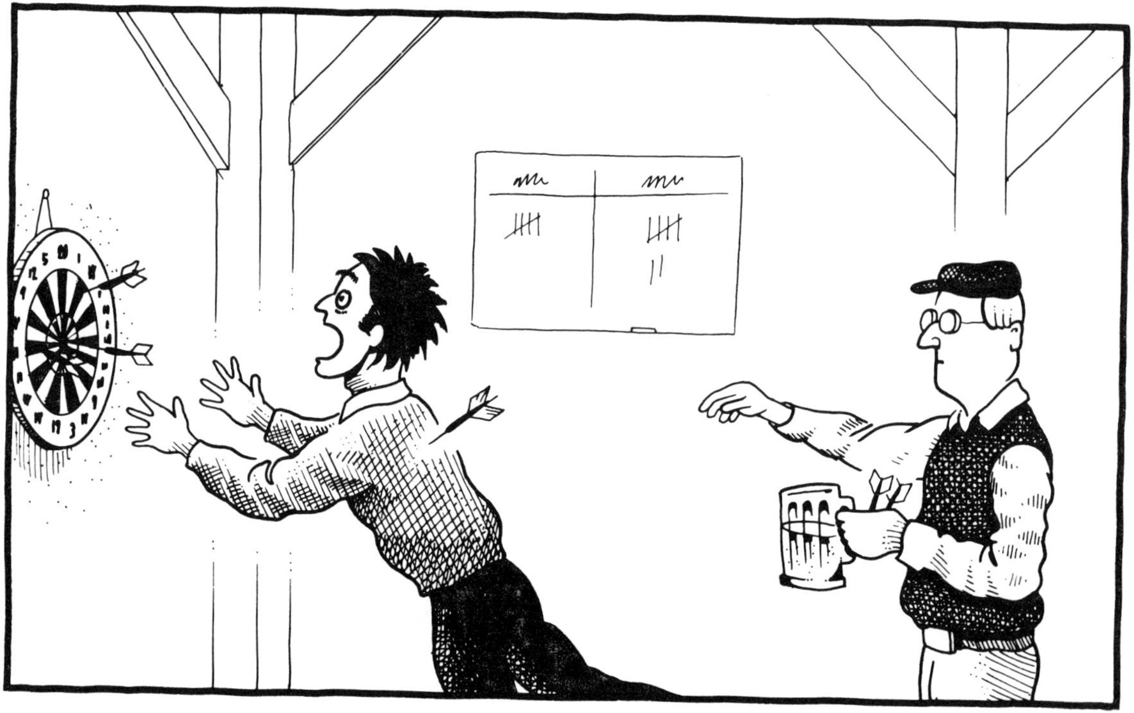

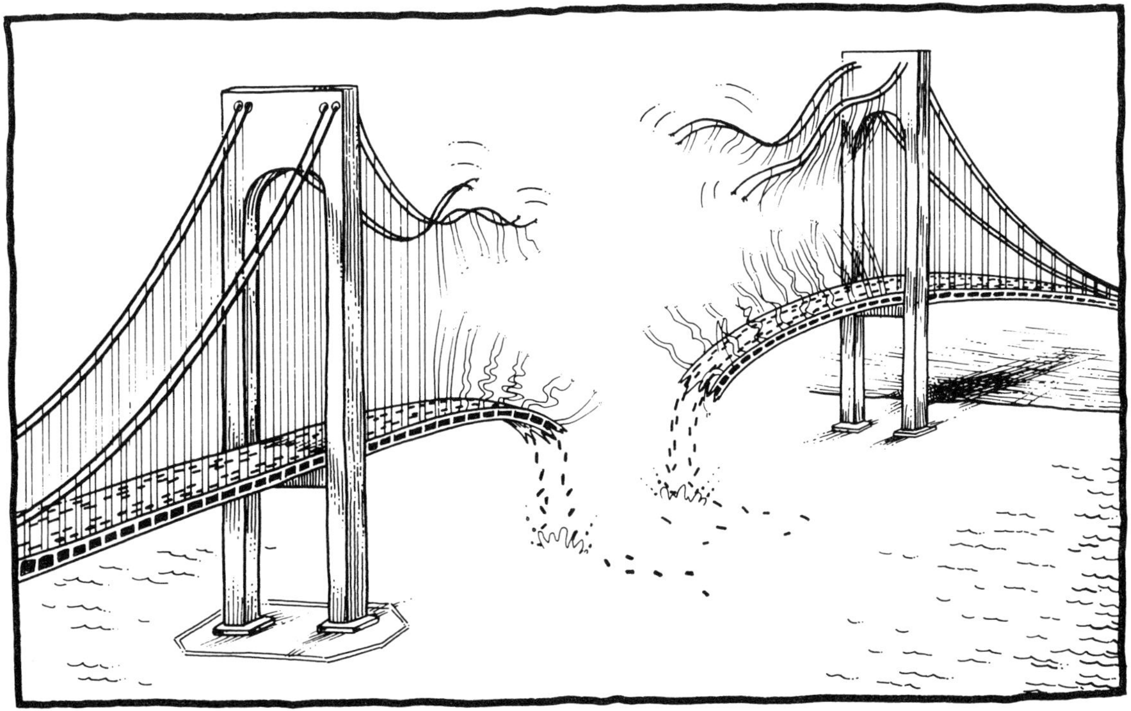

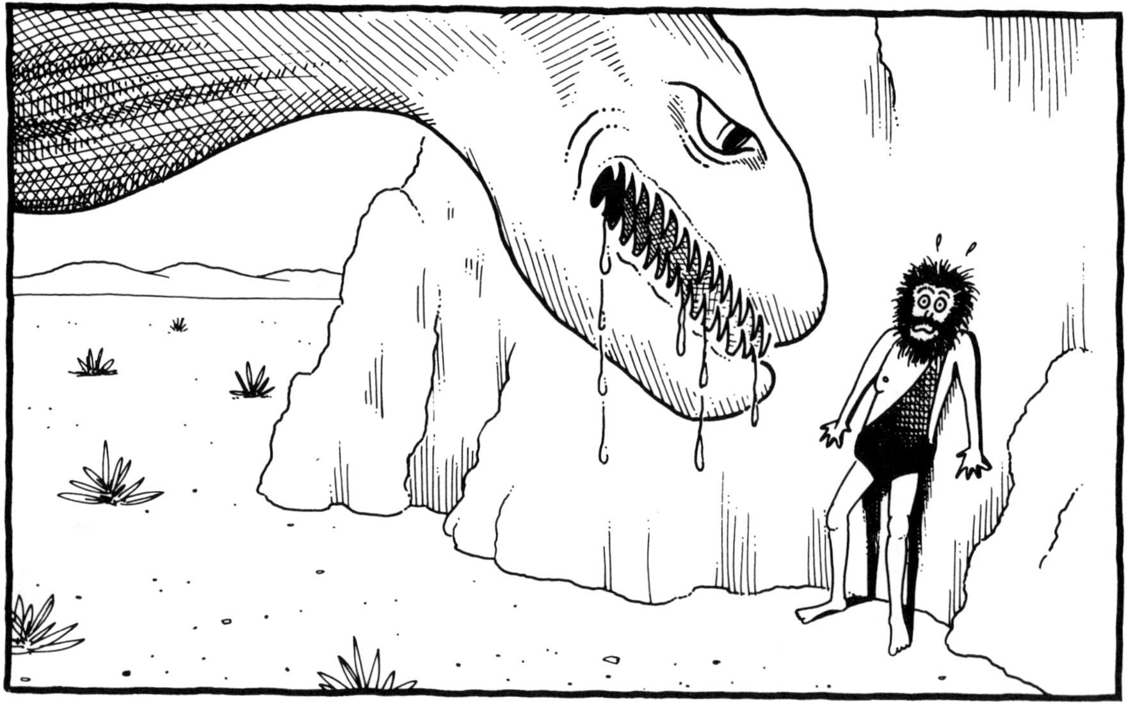

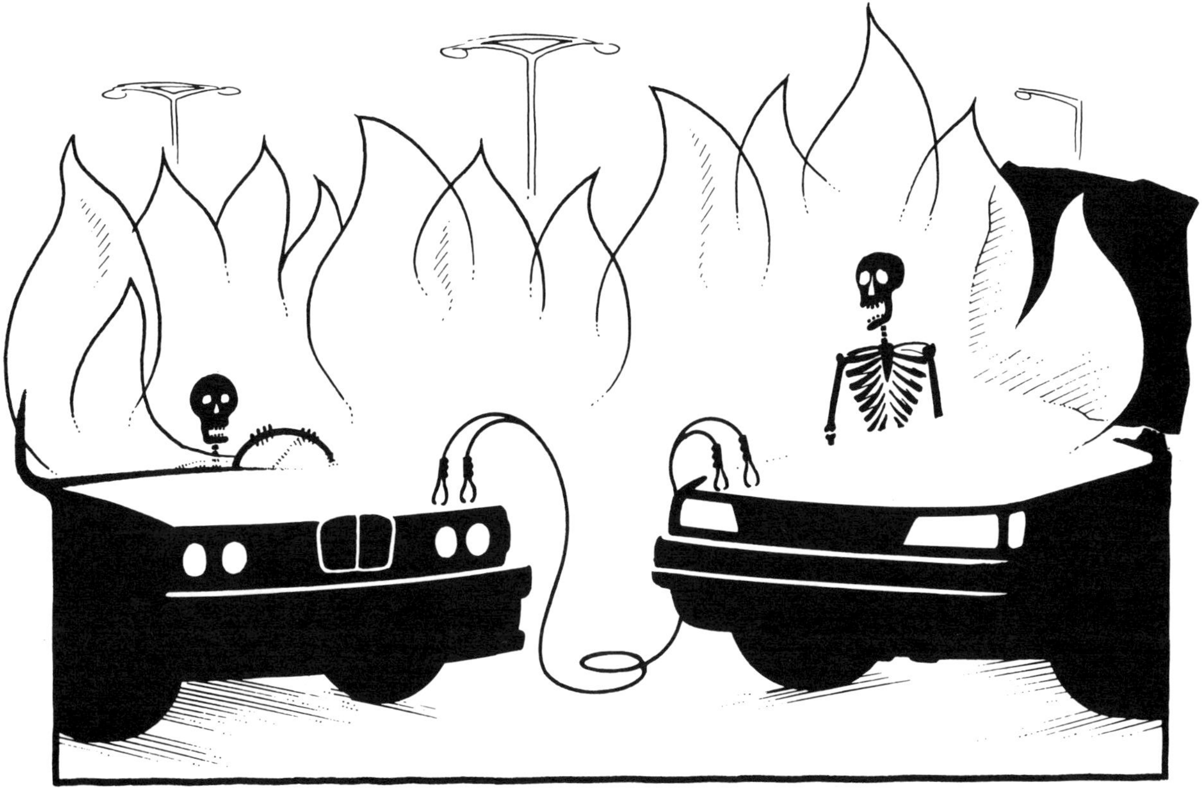

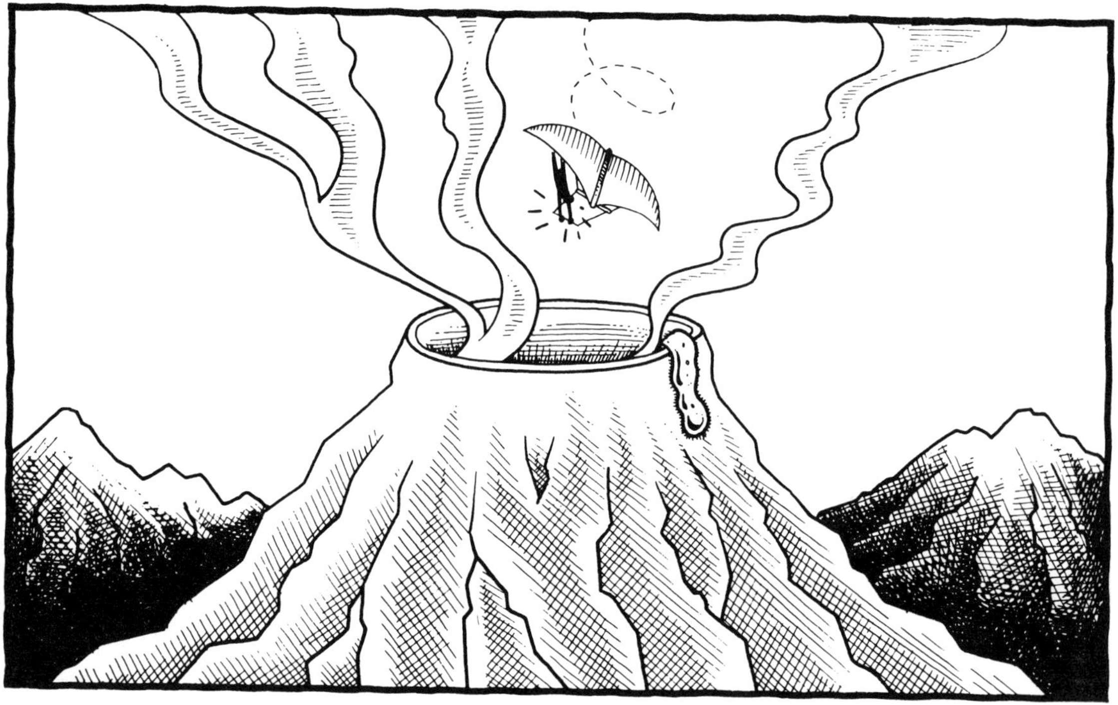

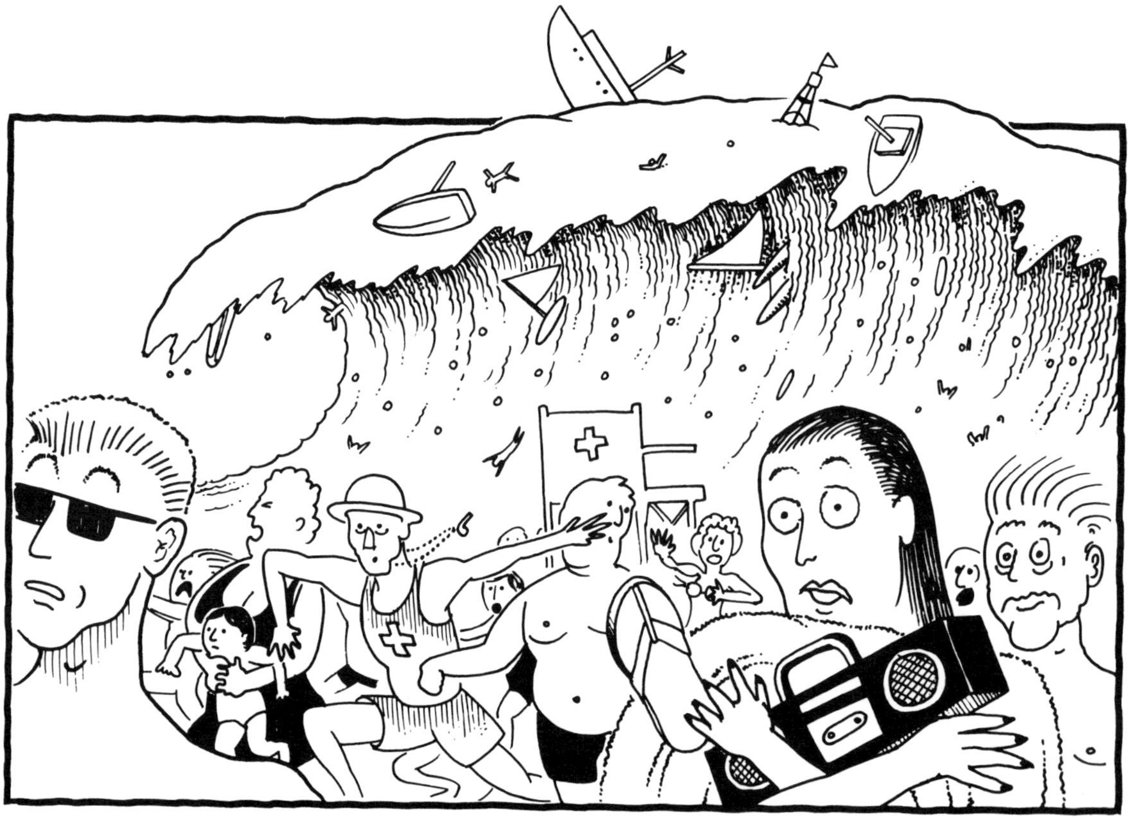

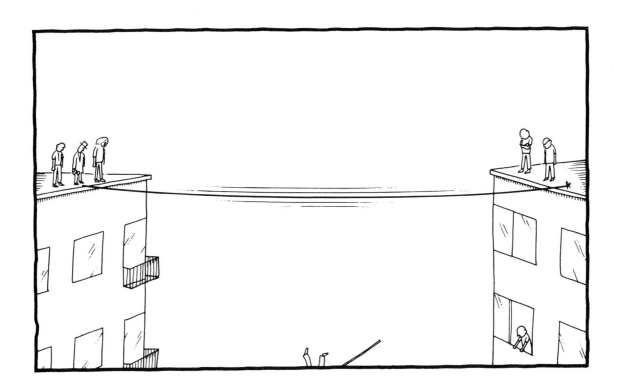

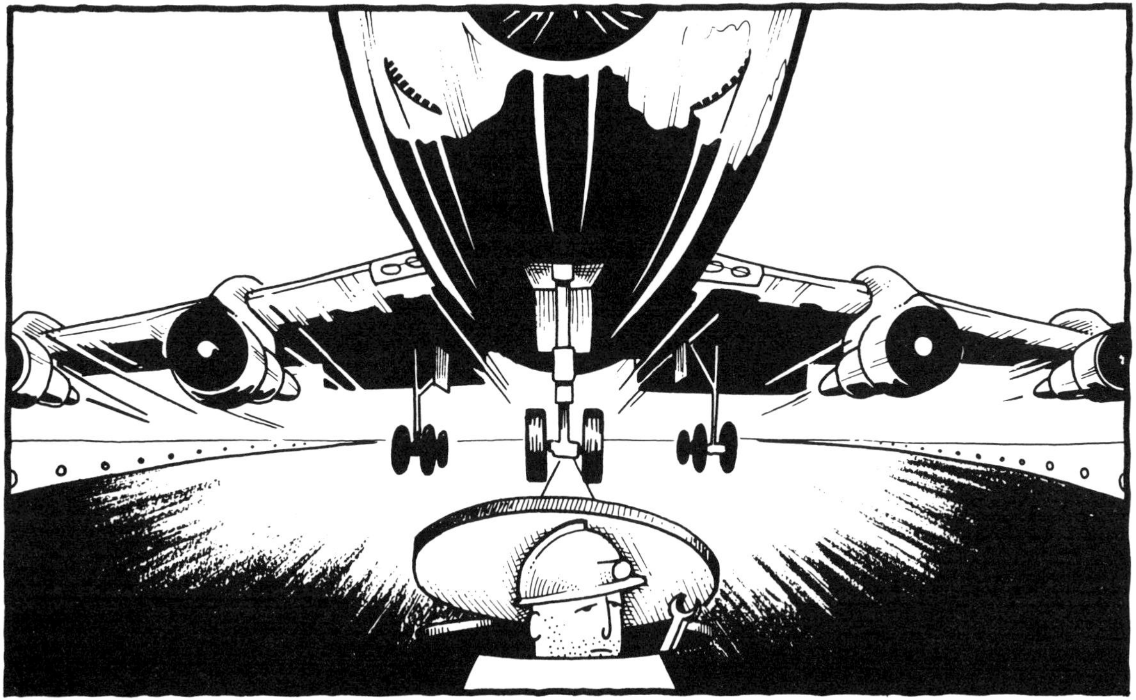

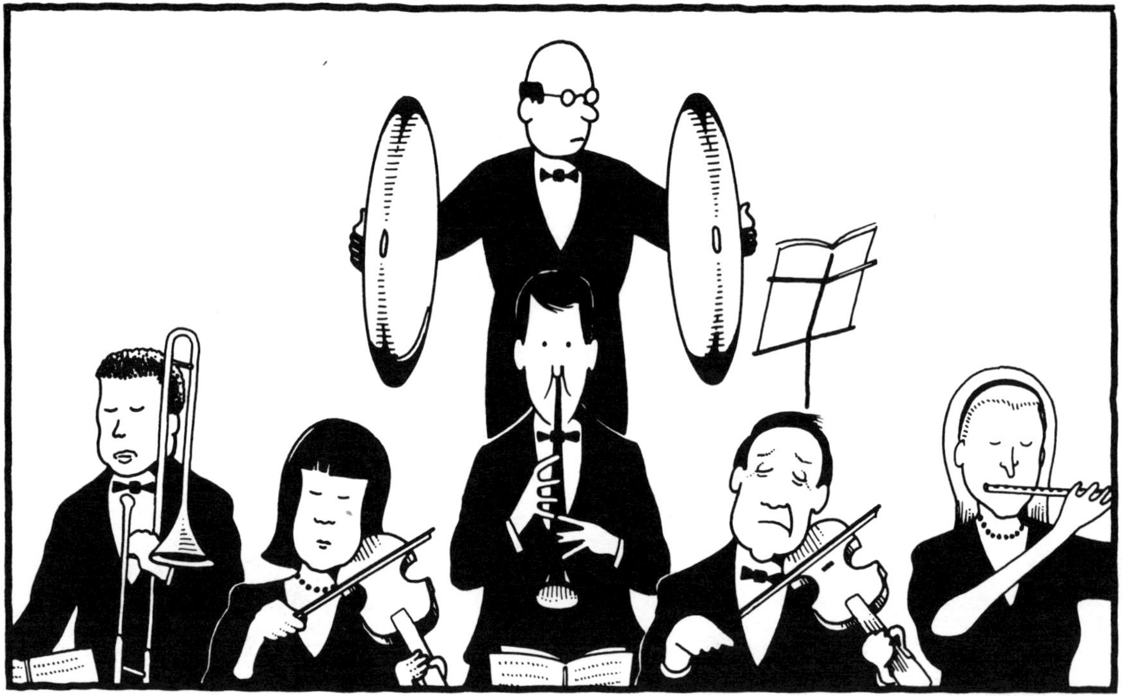

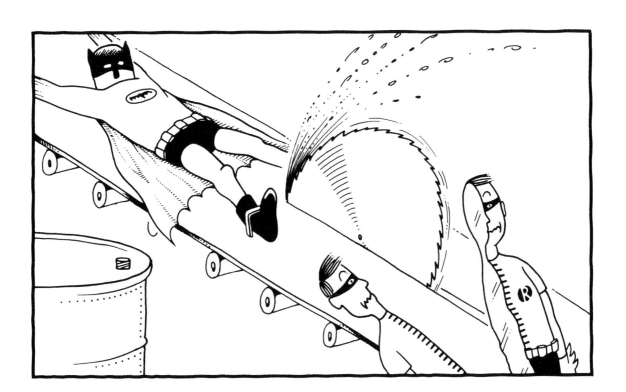

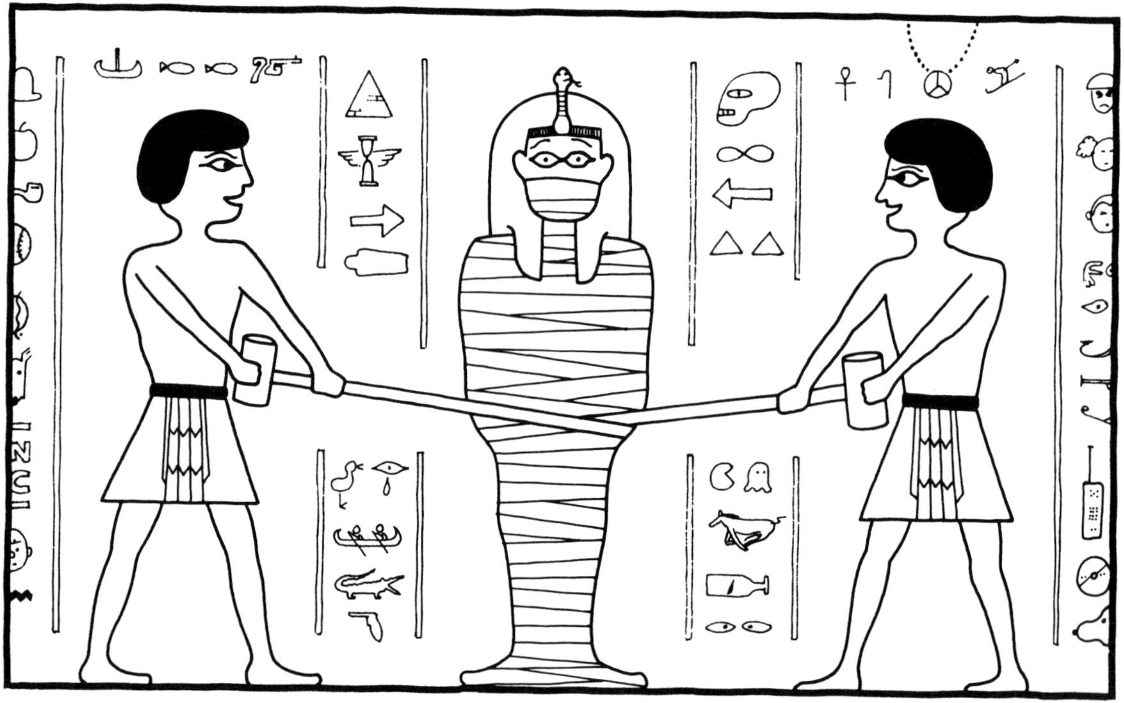

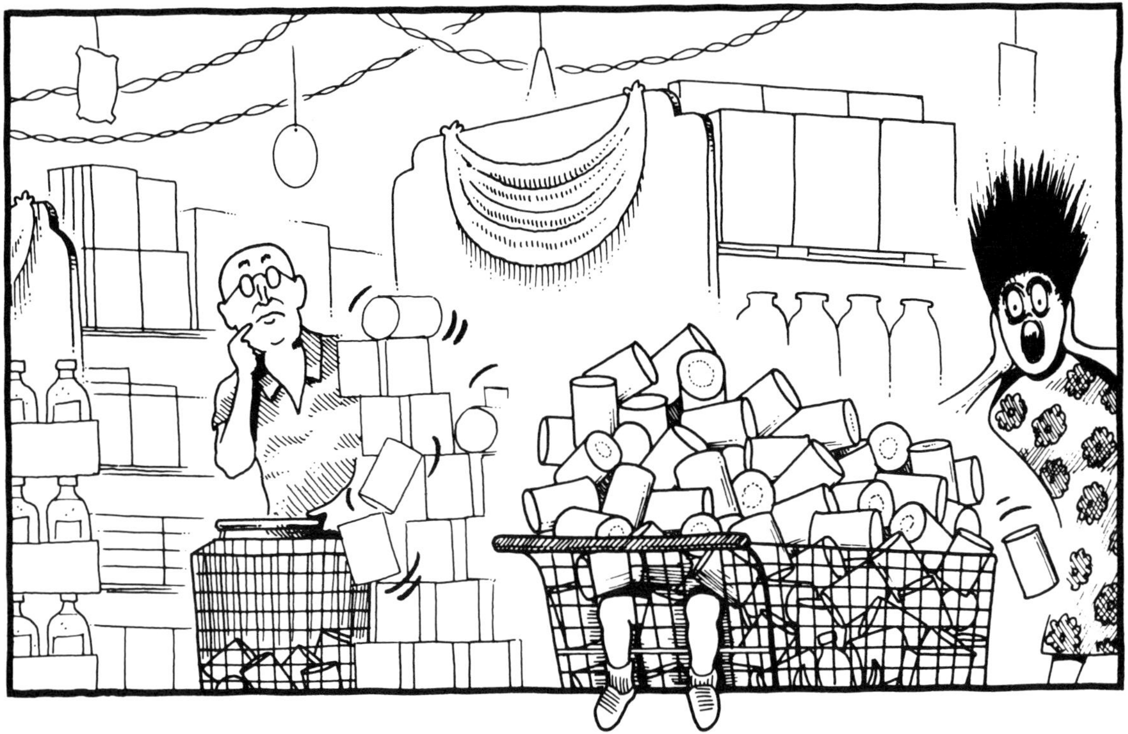

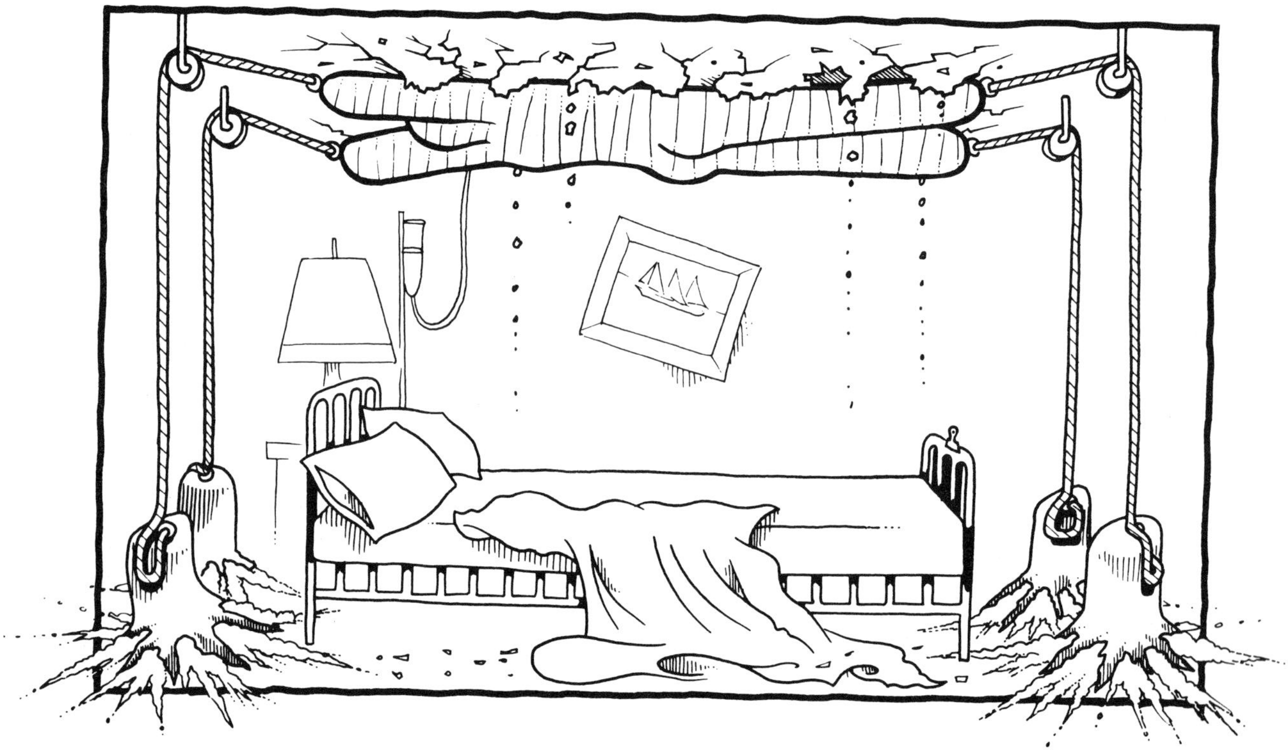

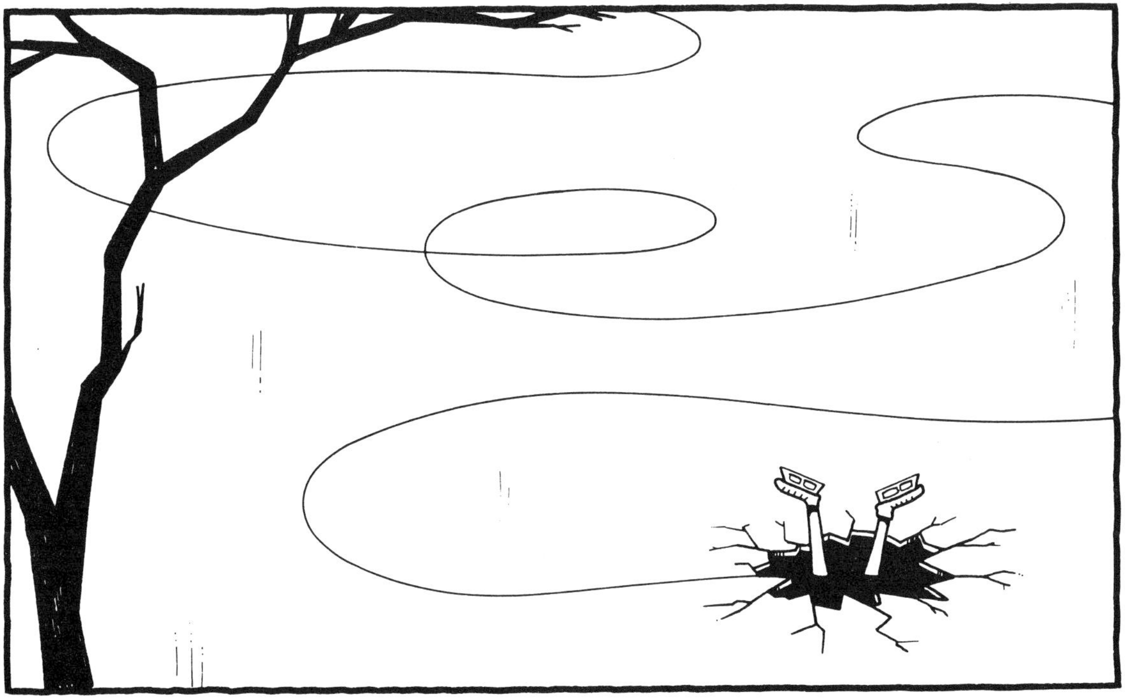

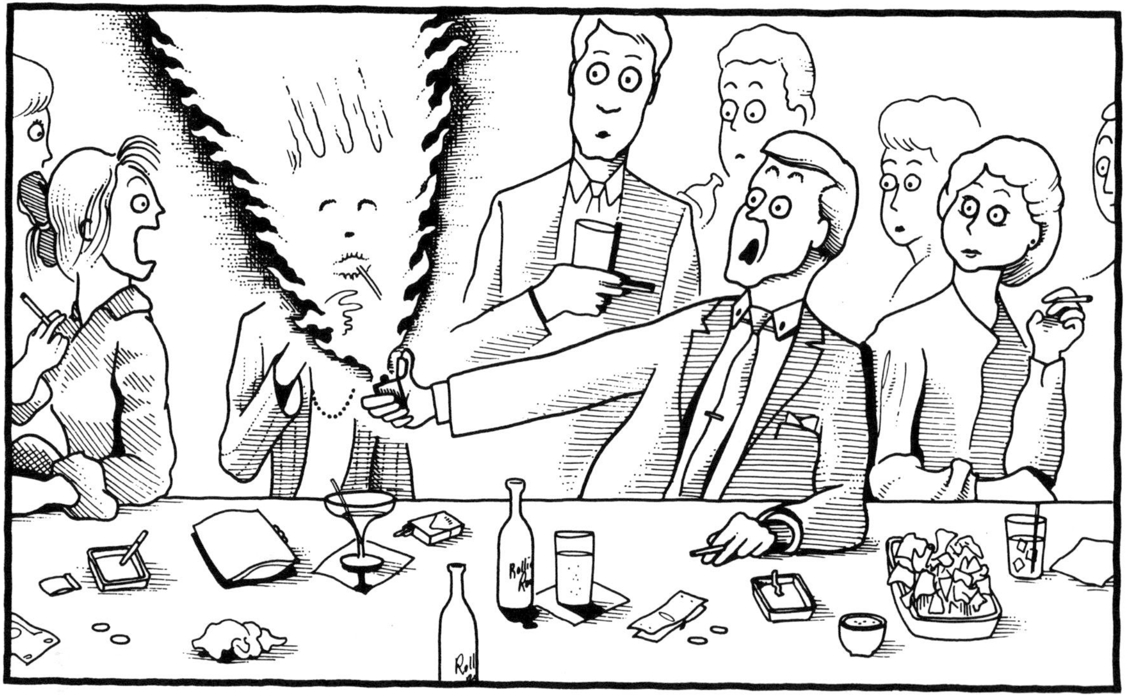

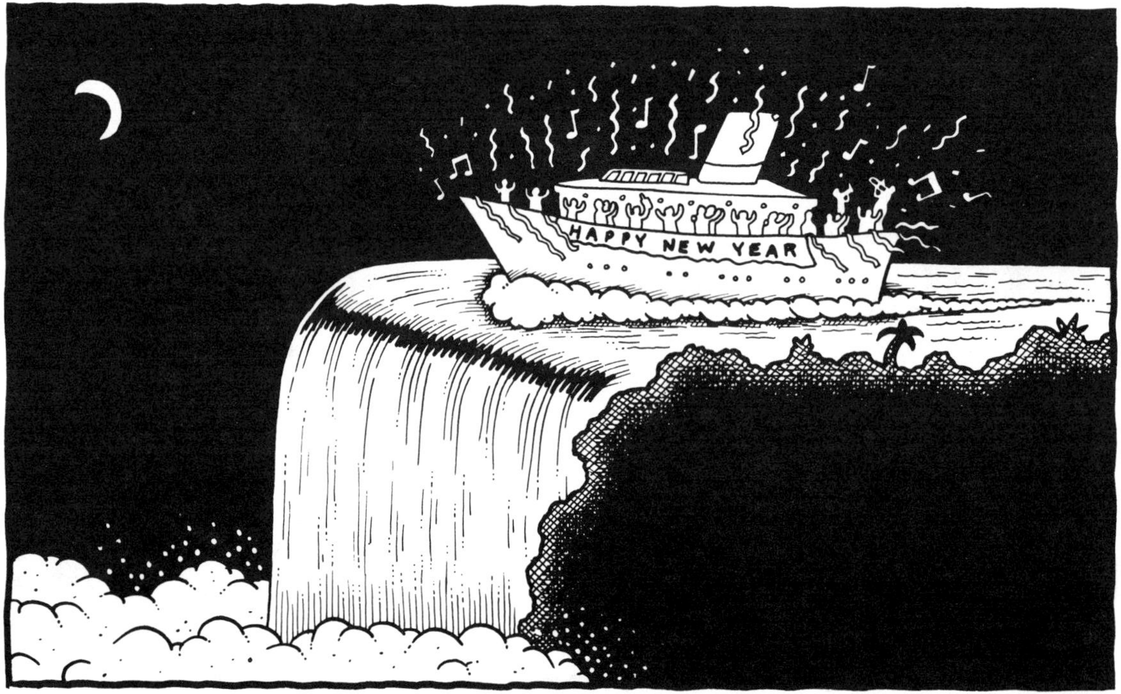
HAPPY NEW YEAR

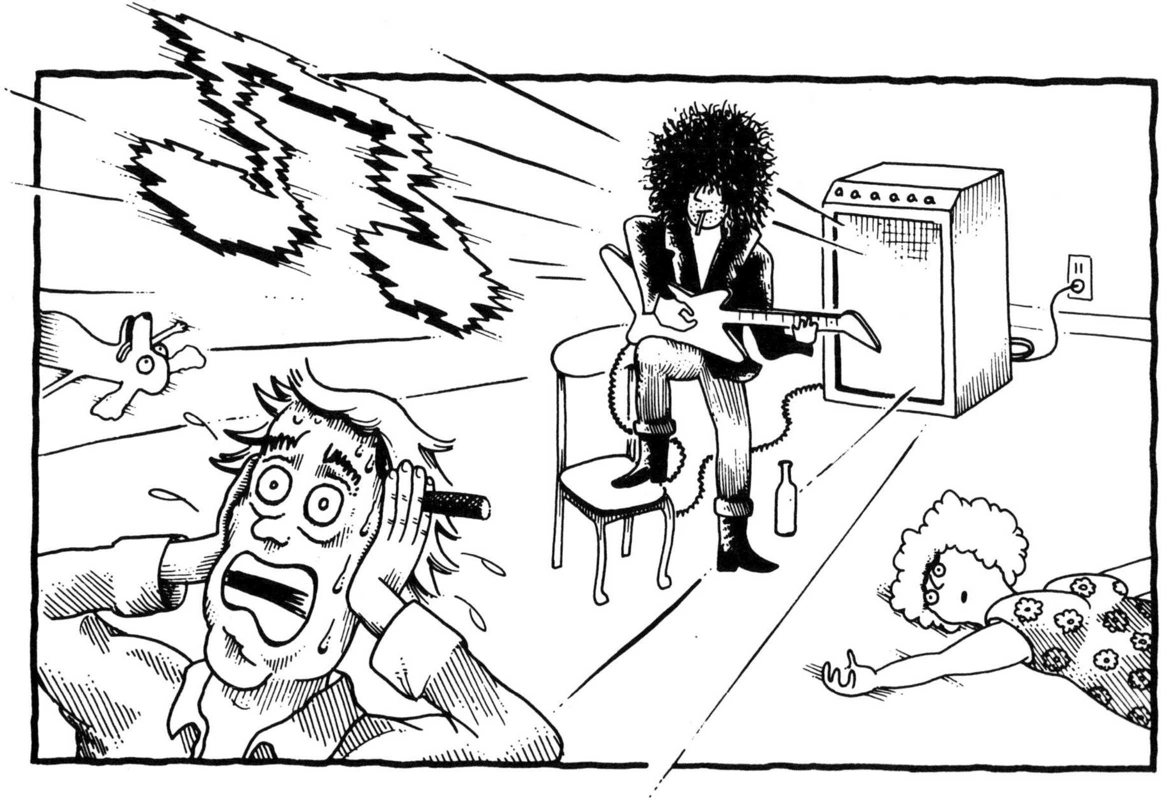

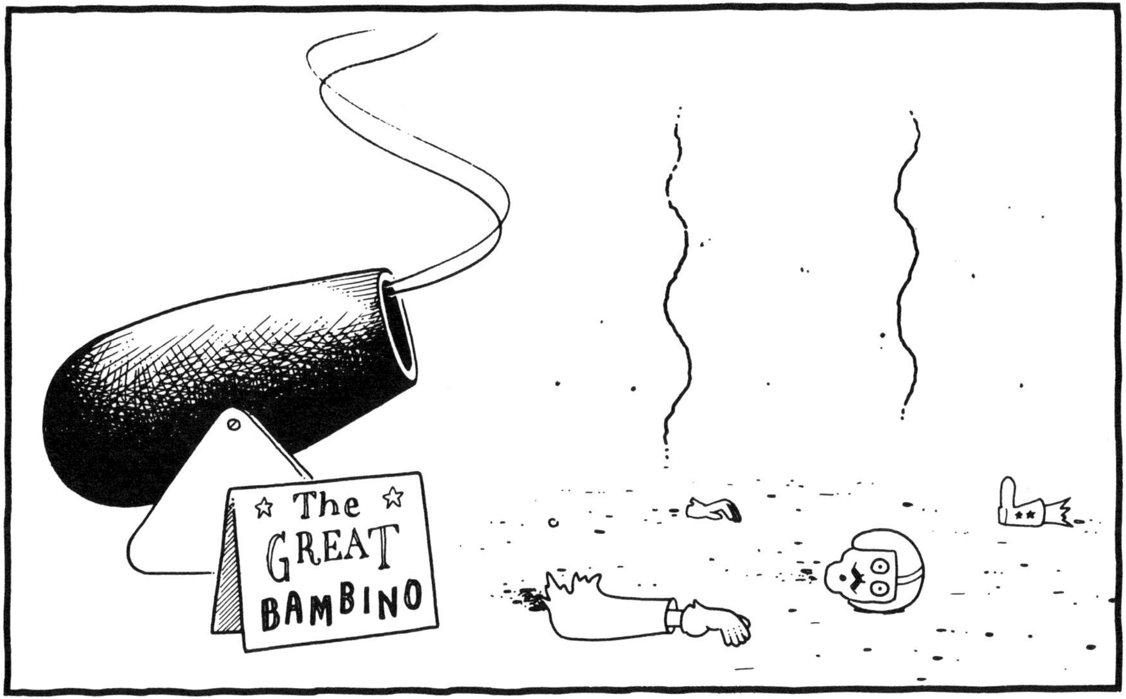
The GREAT BAMBINO

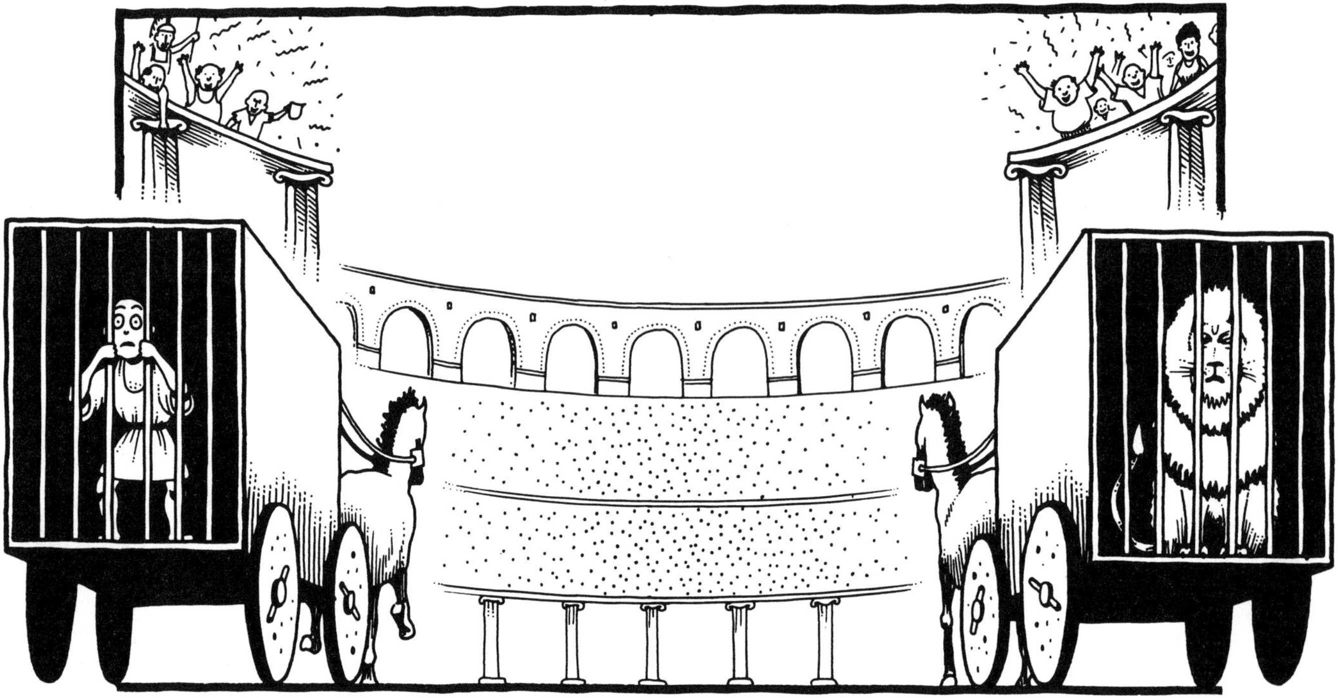

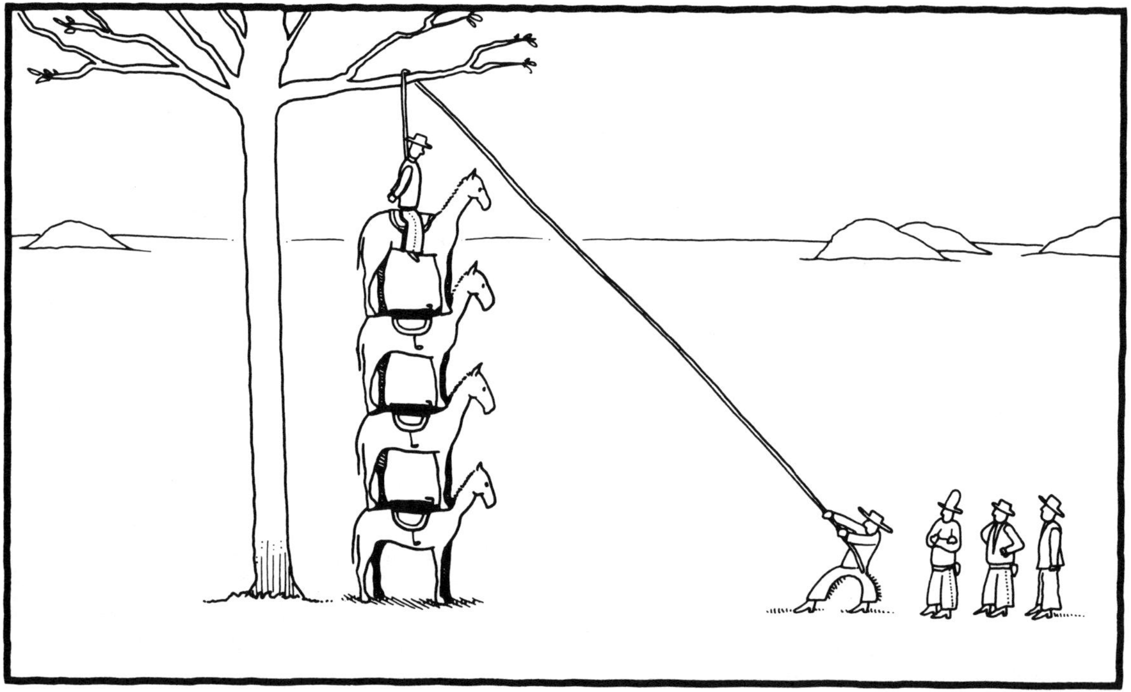

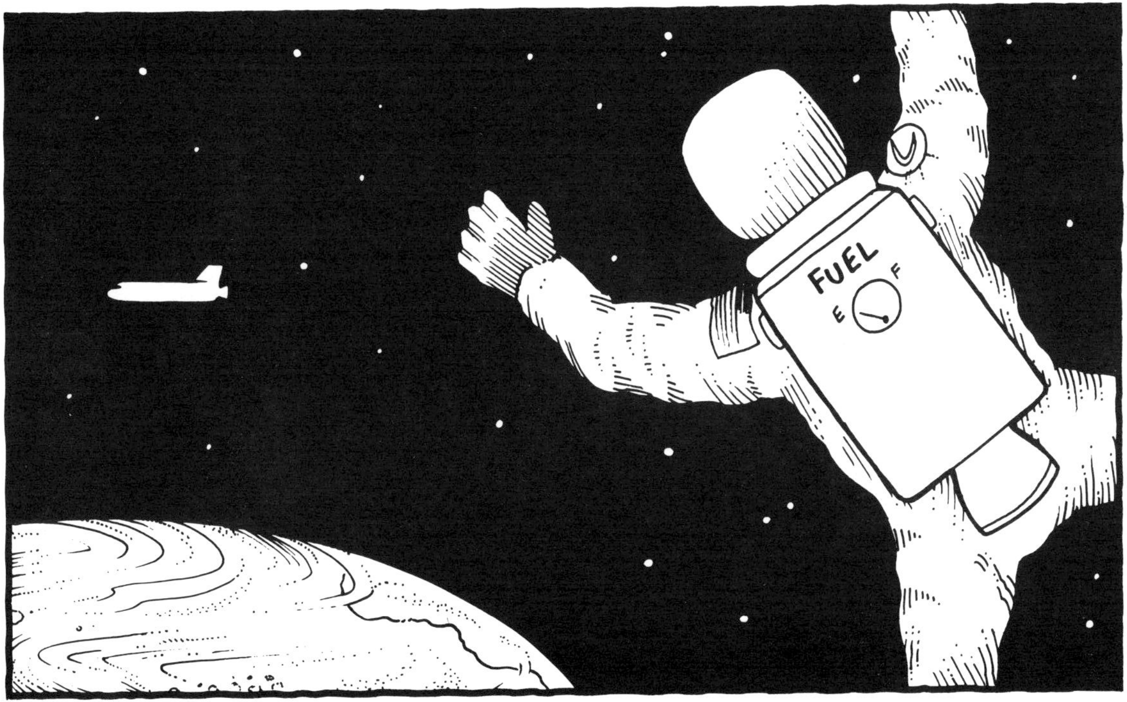

FUEL
E
F

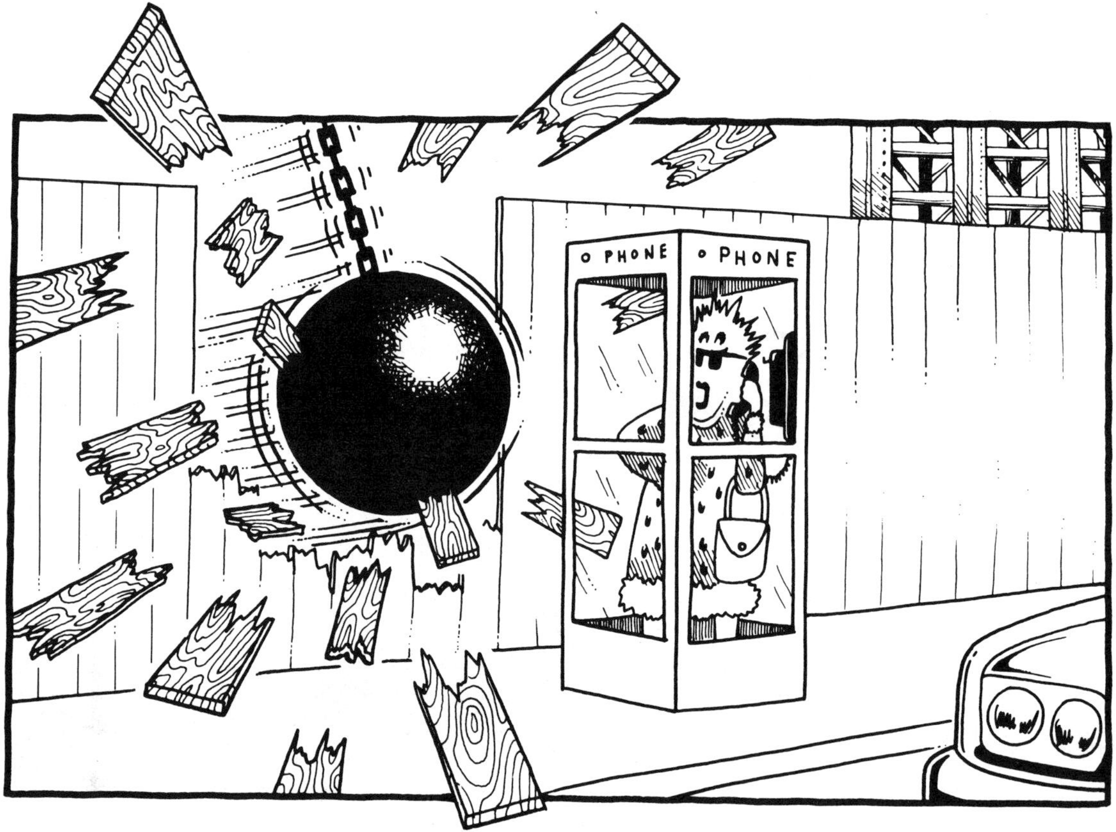
PHONE
PHONE

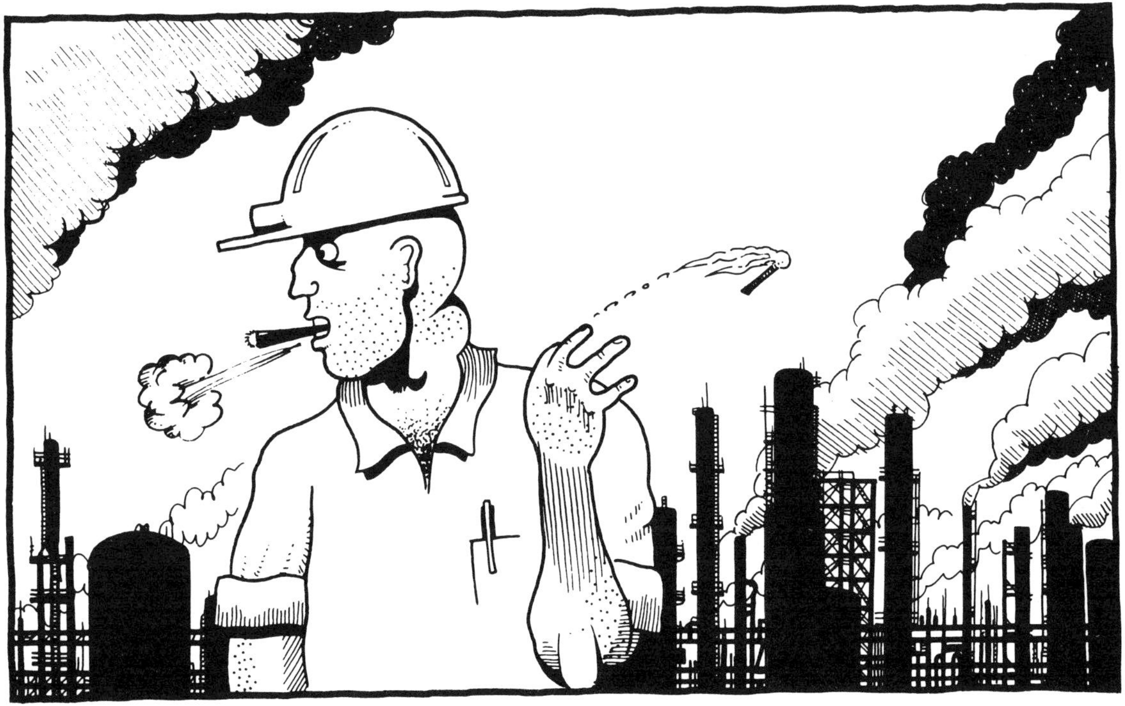

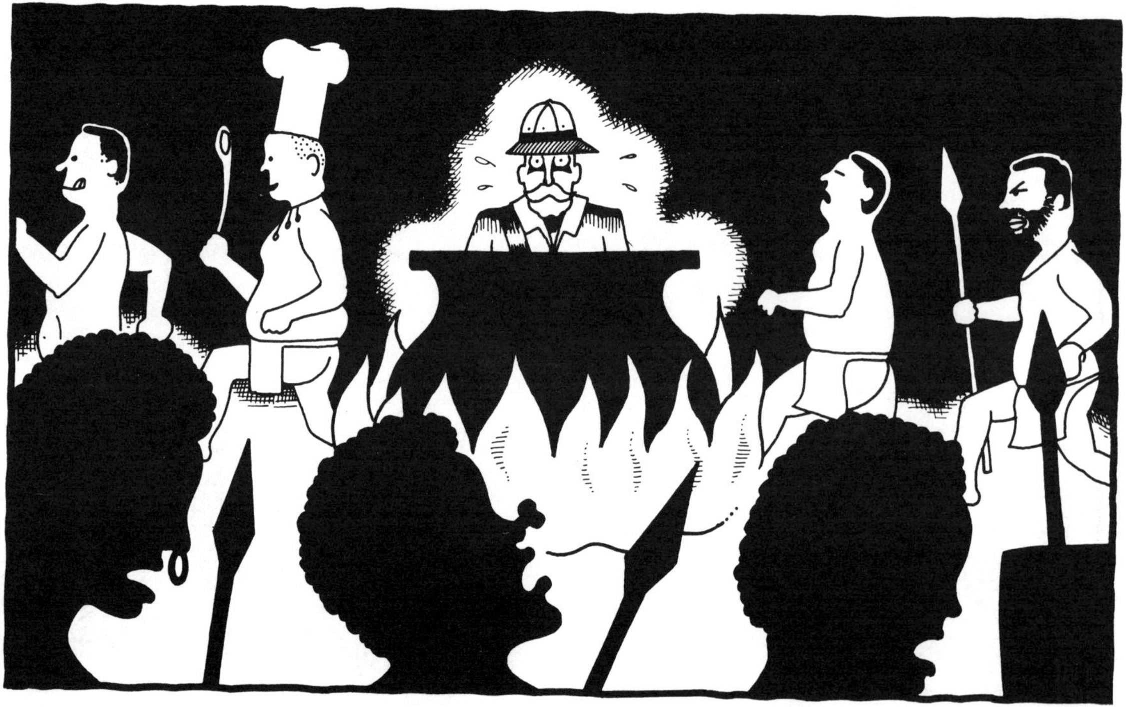

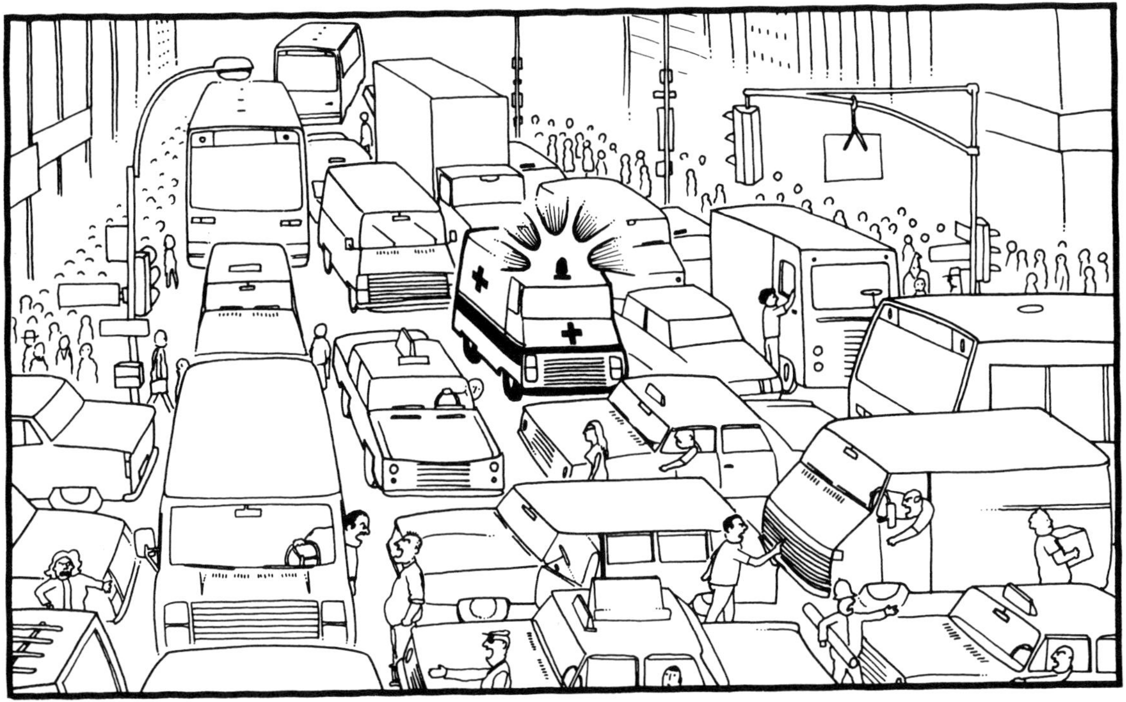

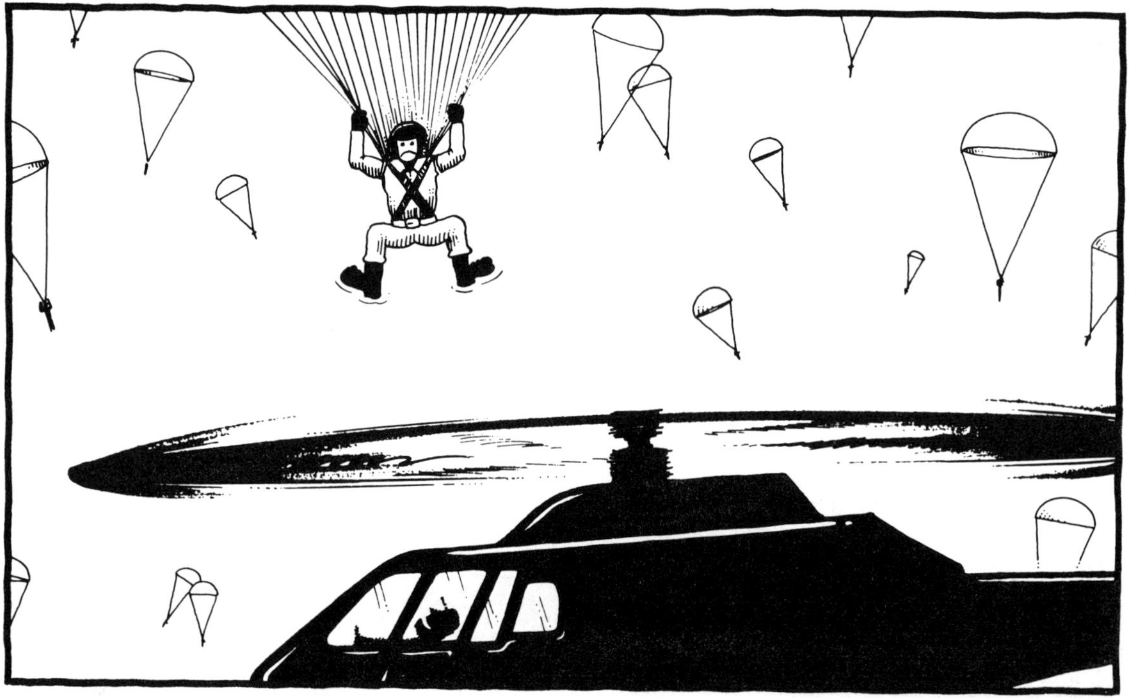

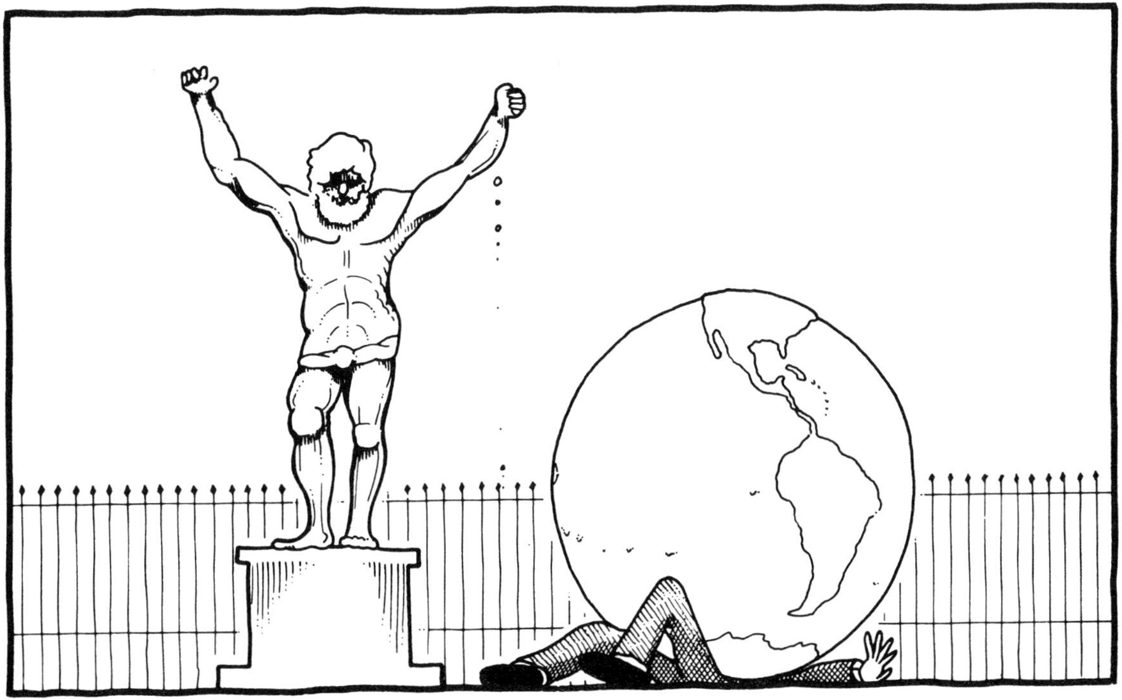

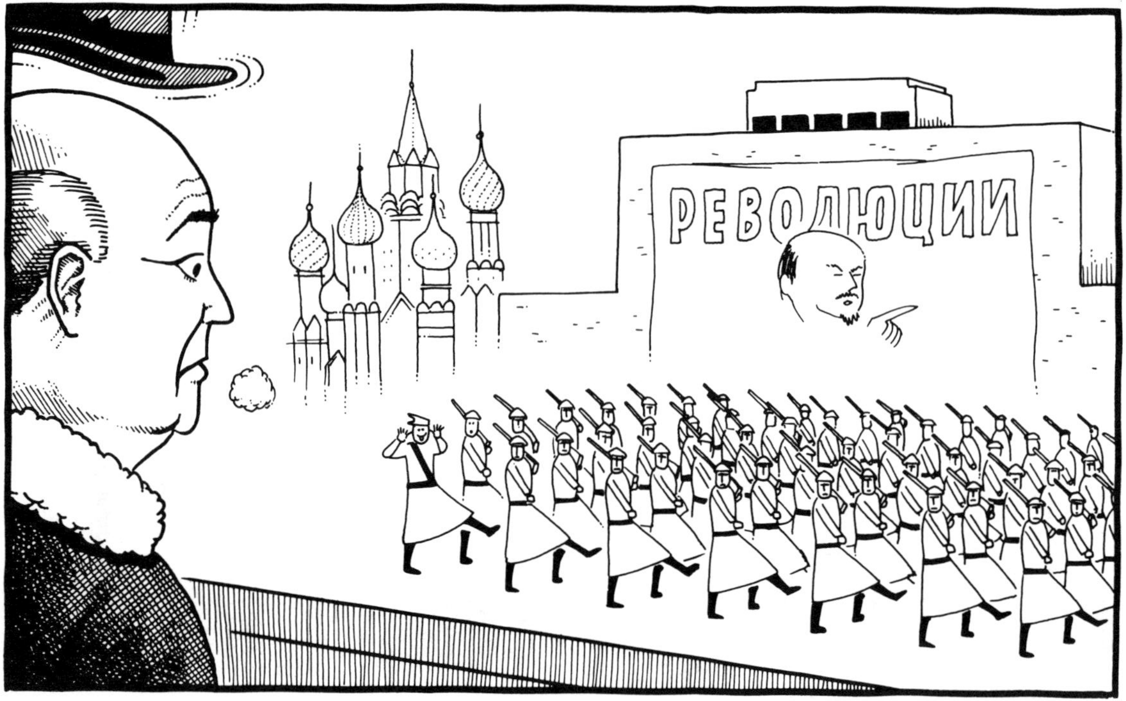
РЕВОЛЮЦИИ

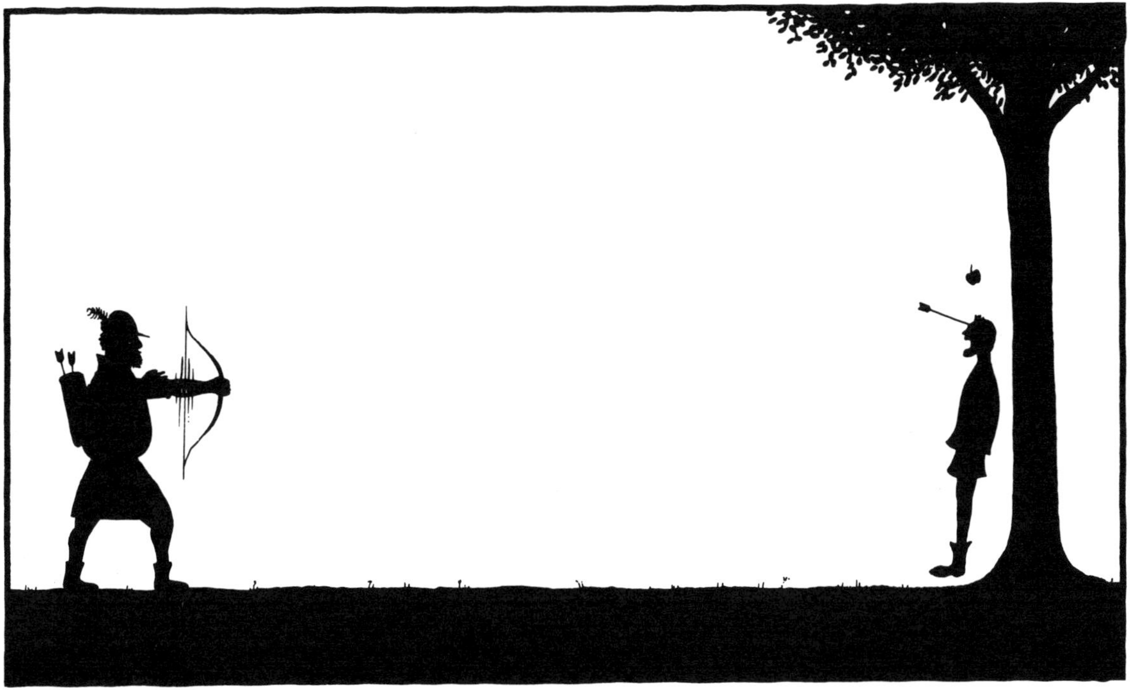

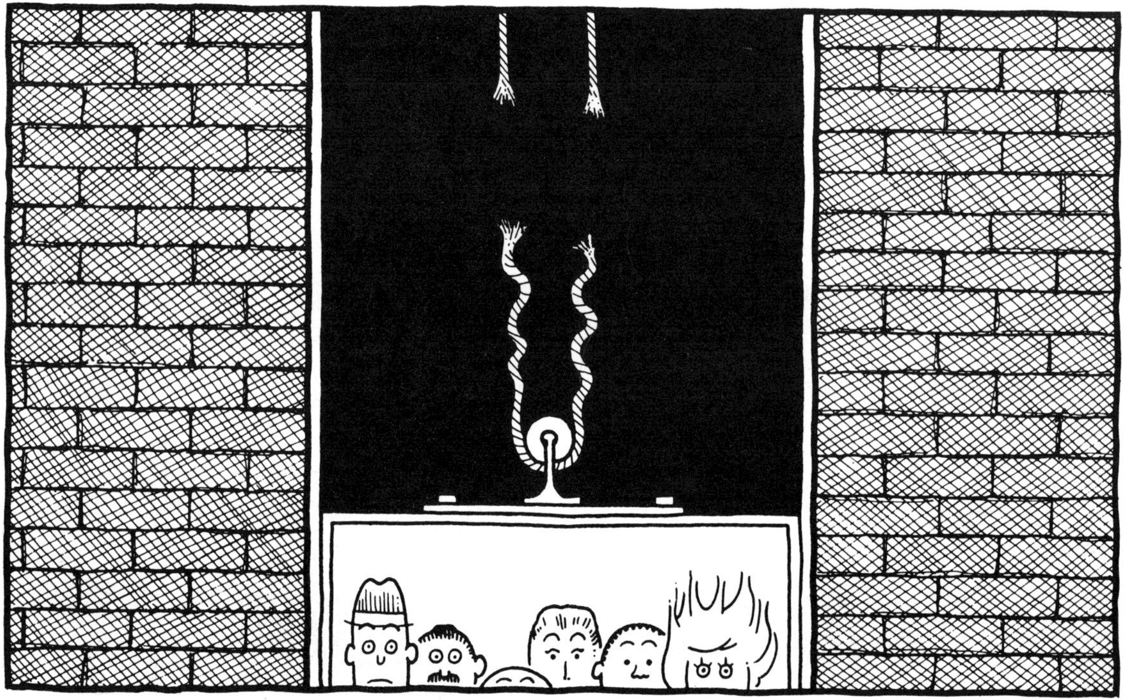

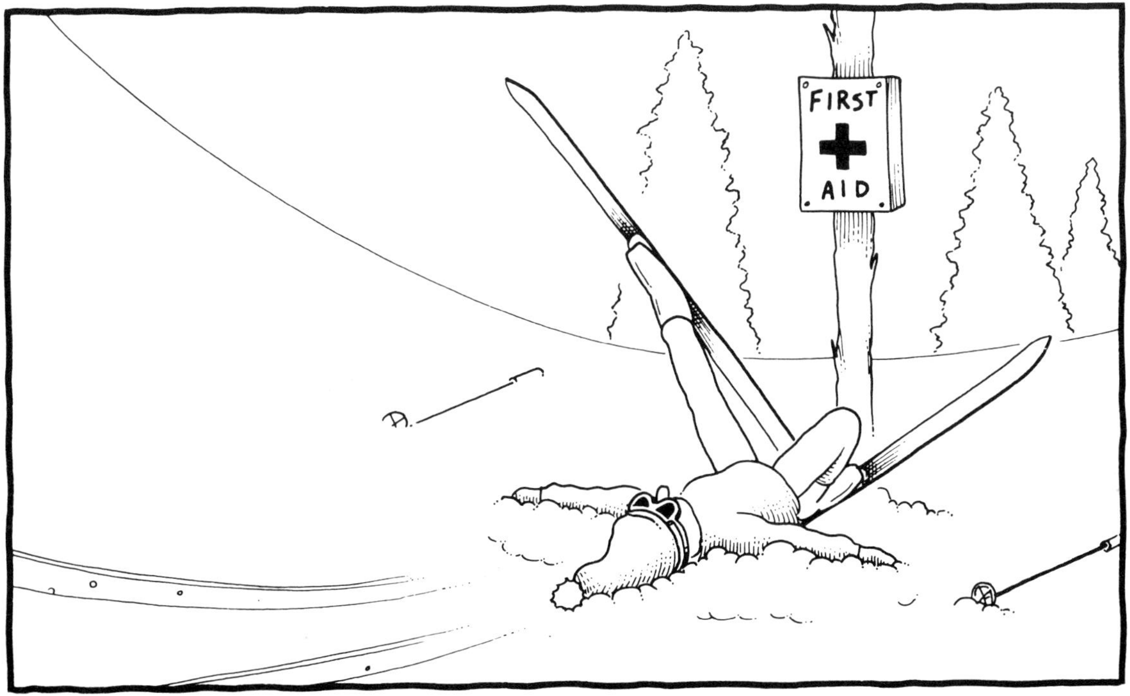
FIRST
AID

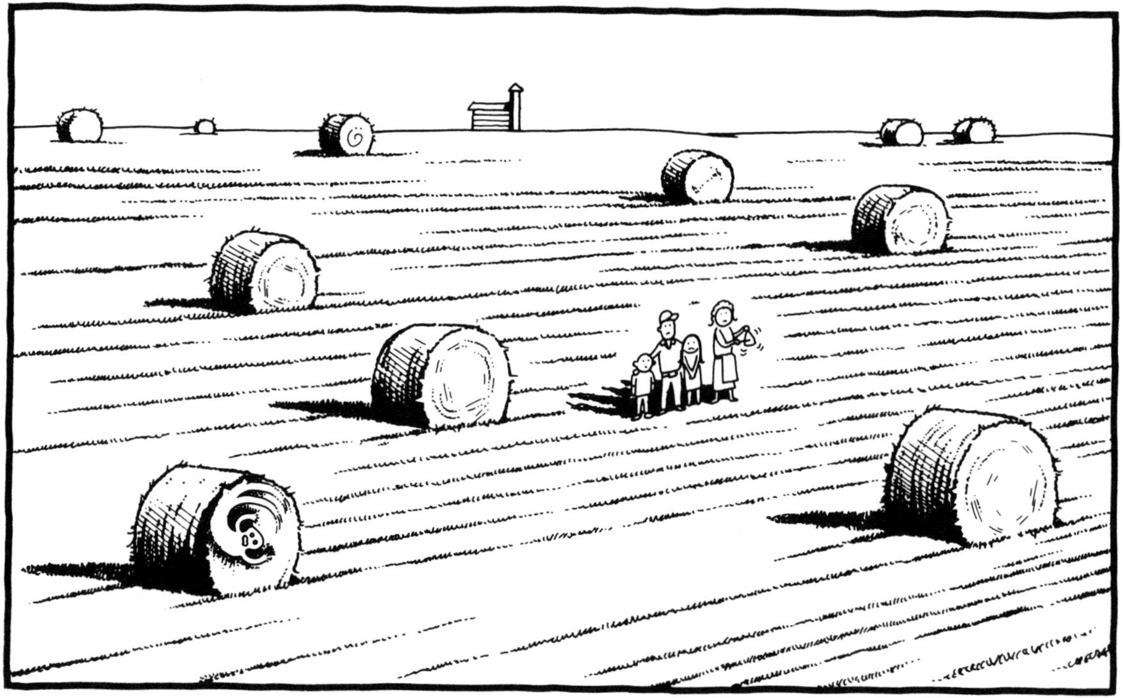

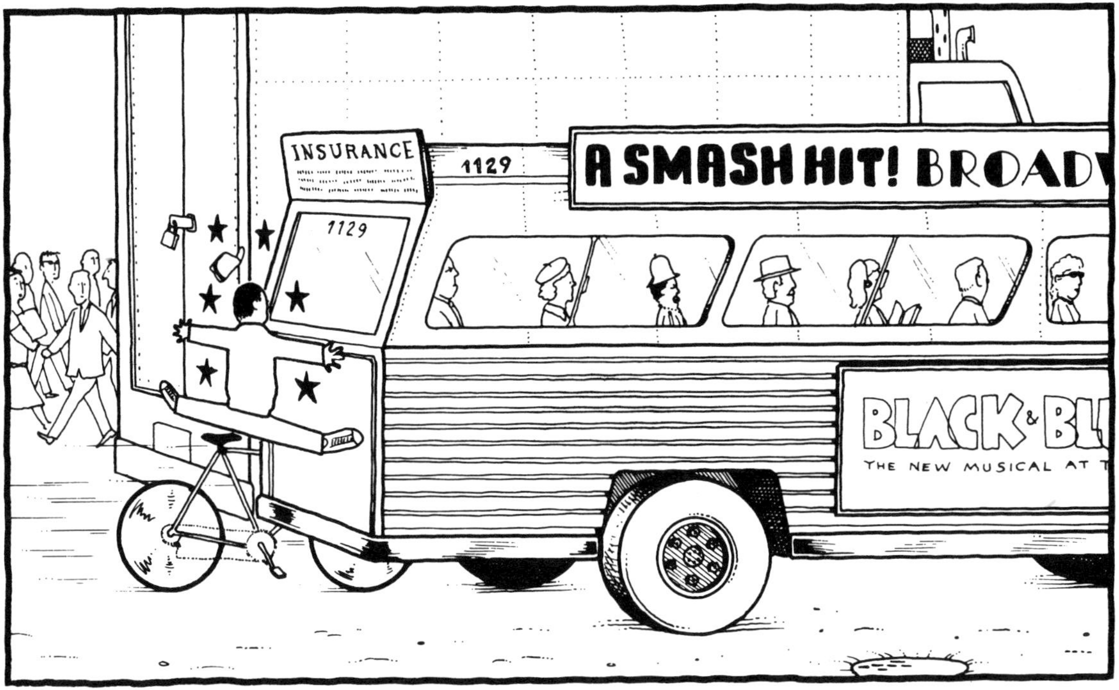
INSURANCE
1129
1129
A SMASH HIT! BROAD
BLACK&BL
THE NEW MUSICAL AT T

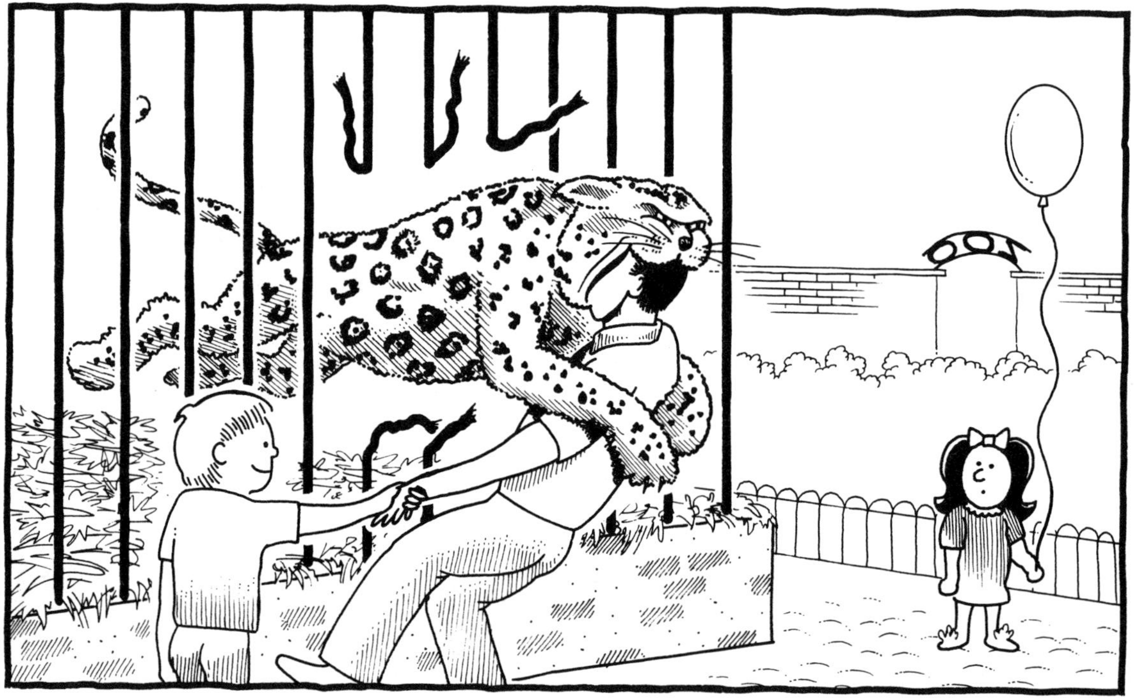

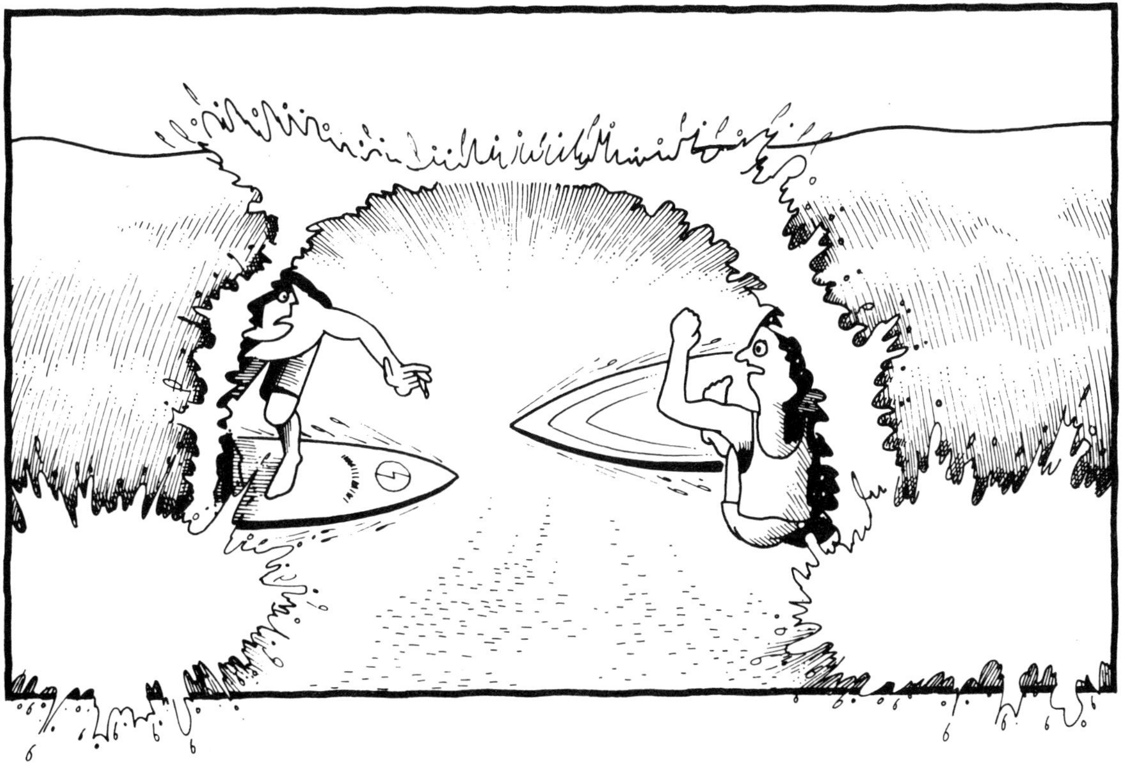

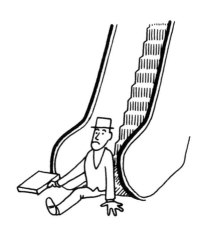 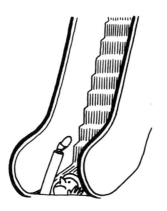 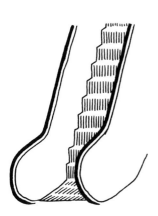

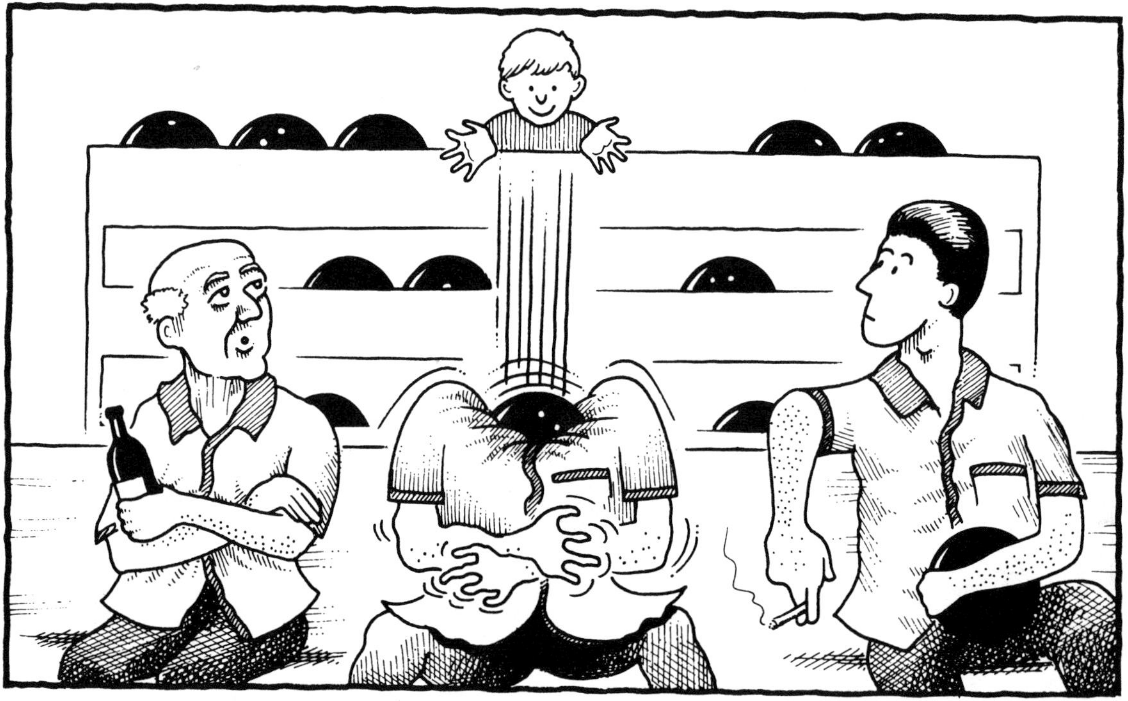

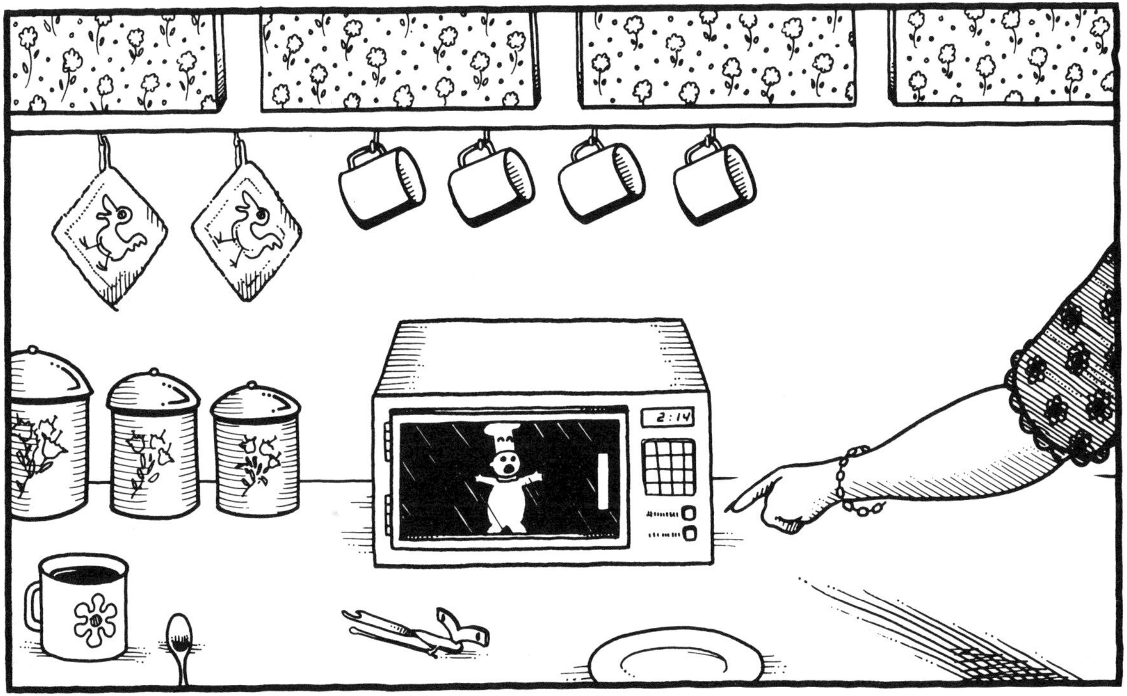
2:14

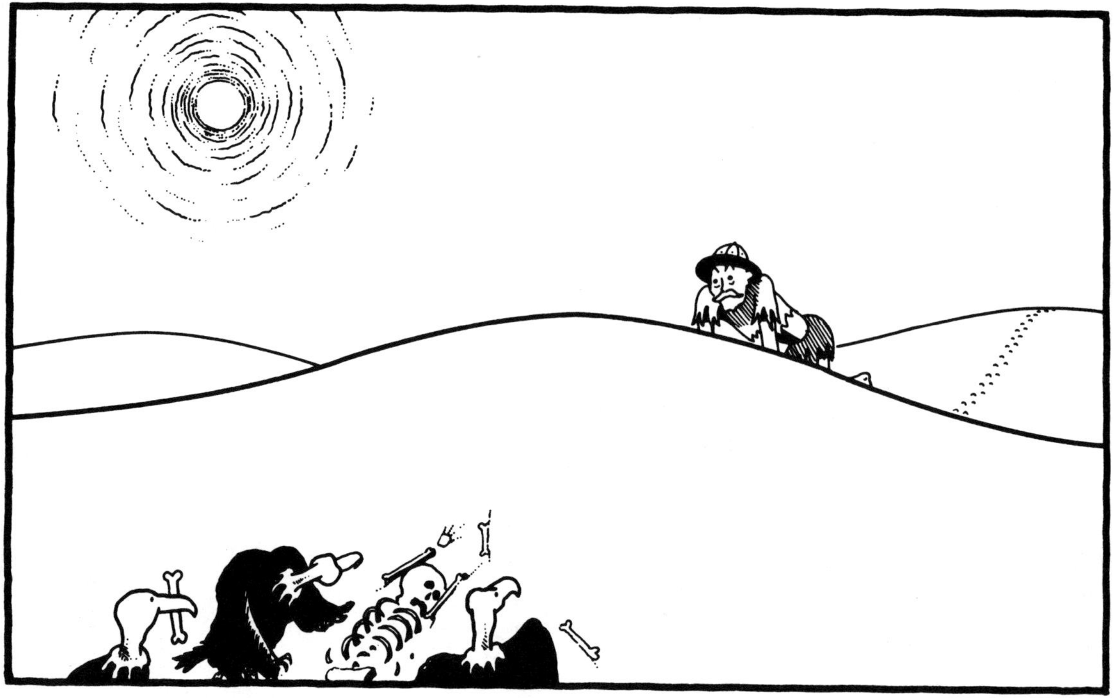

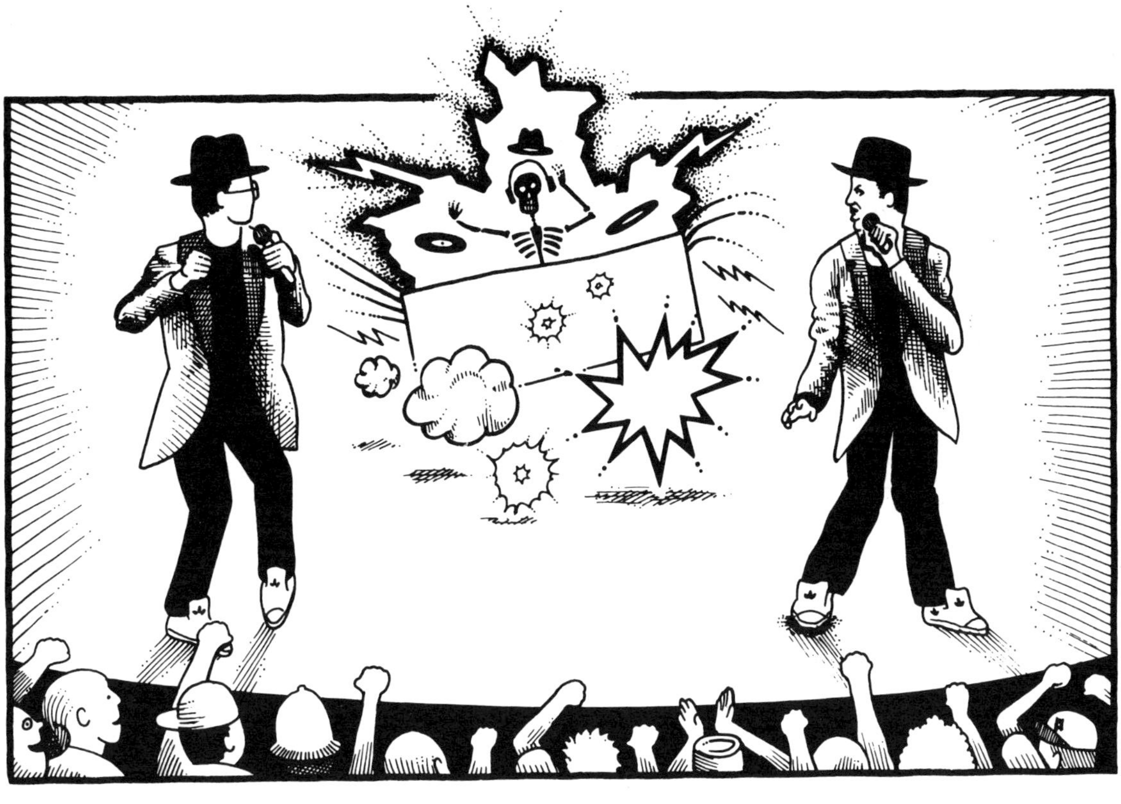

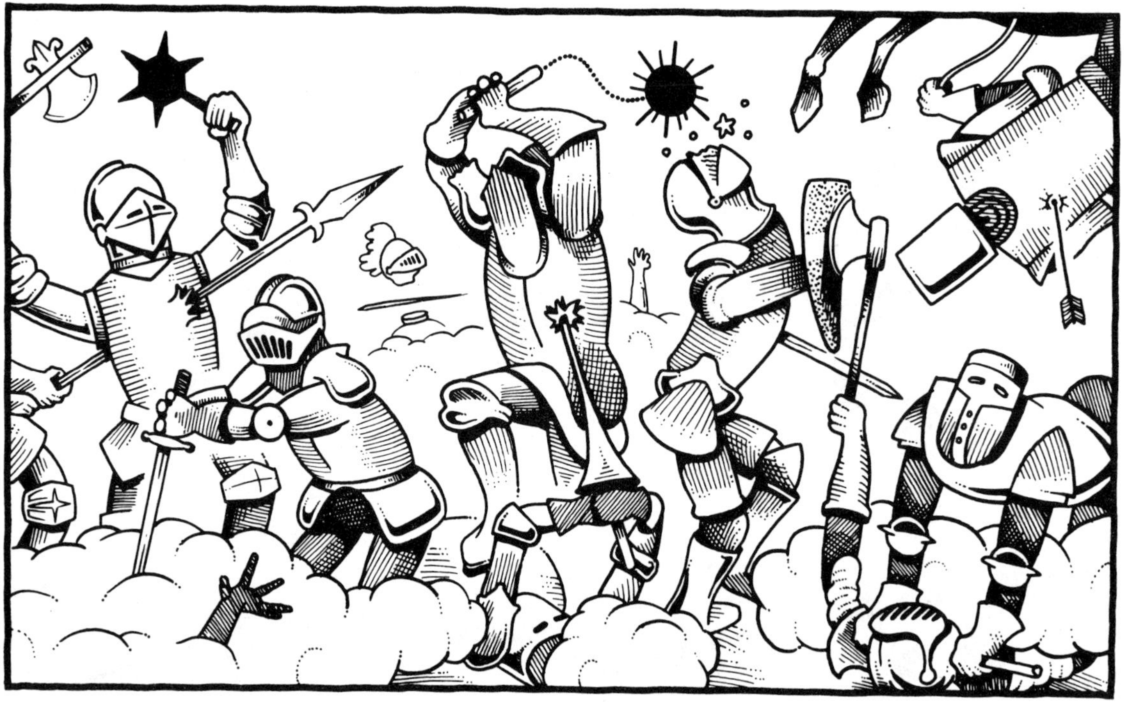

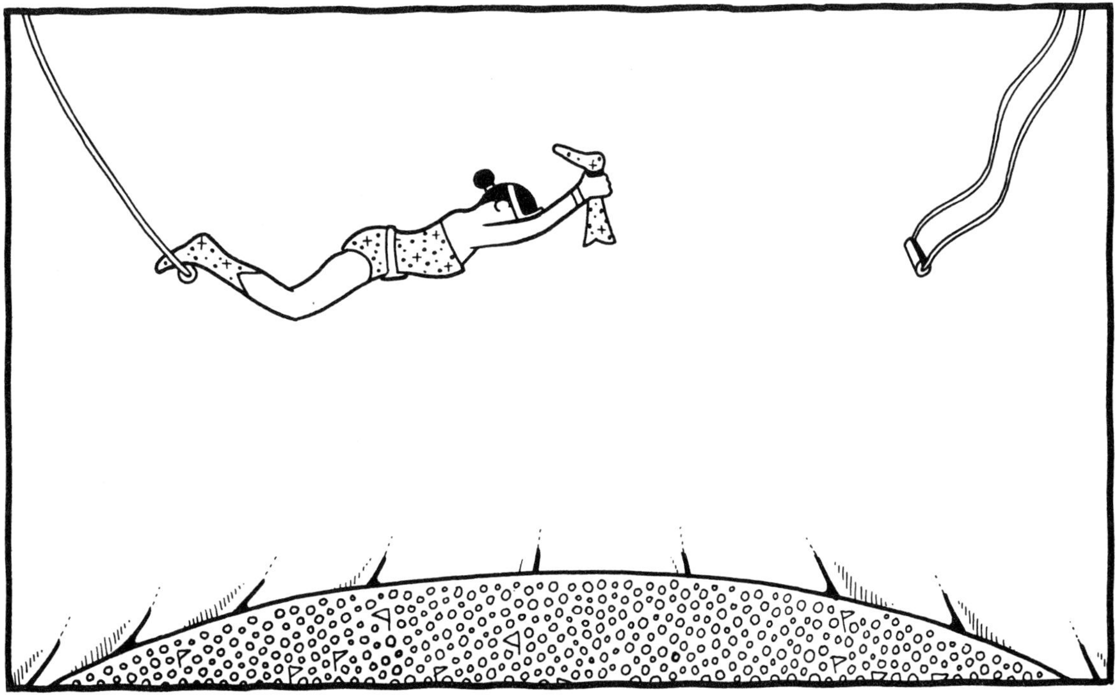

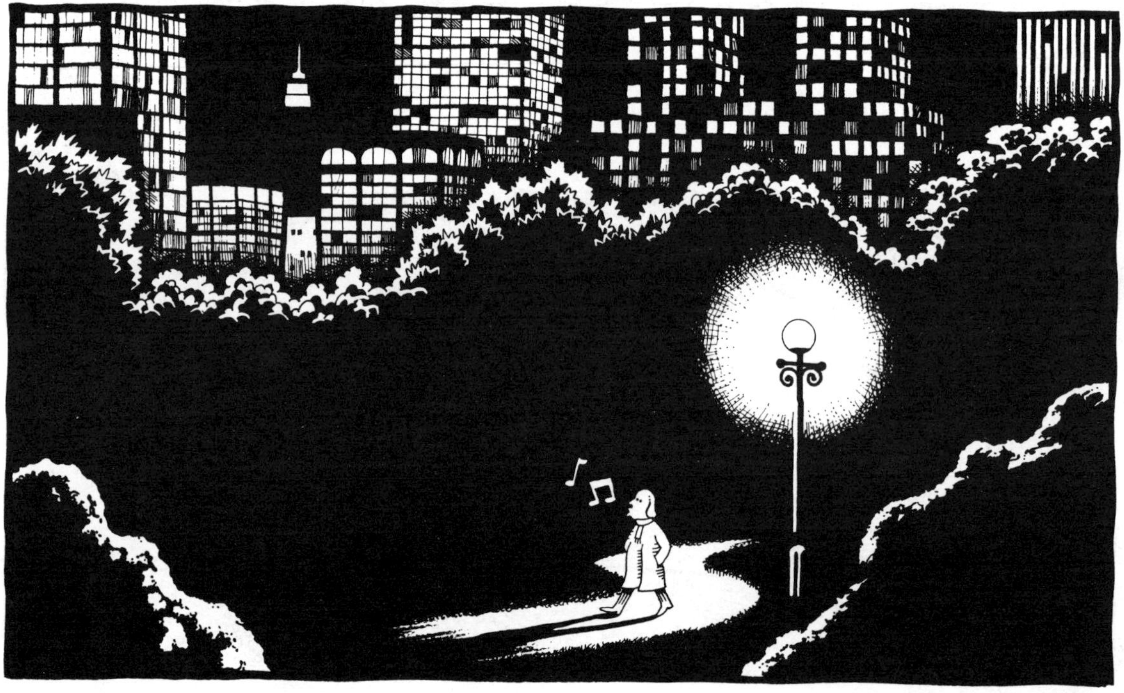

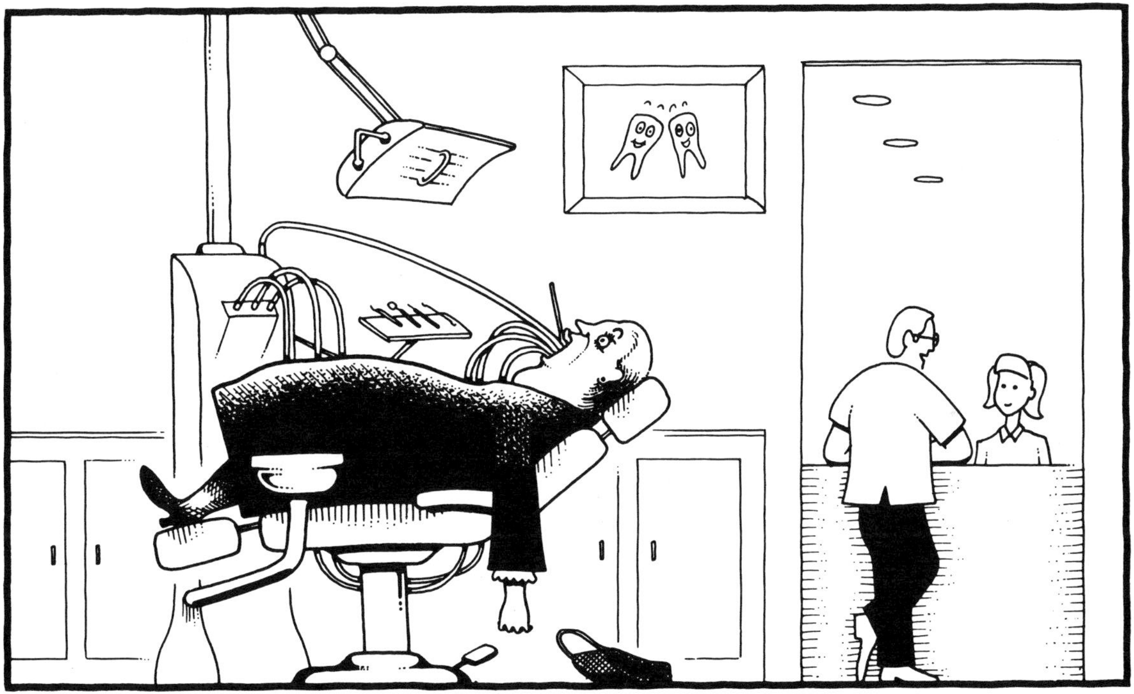

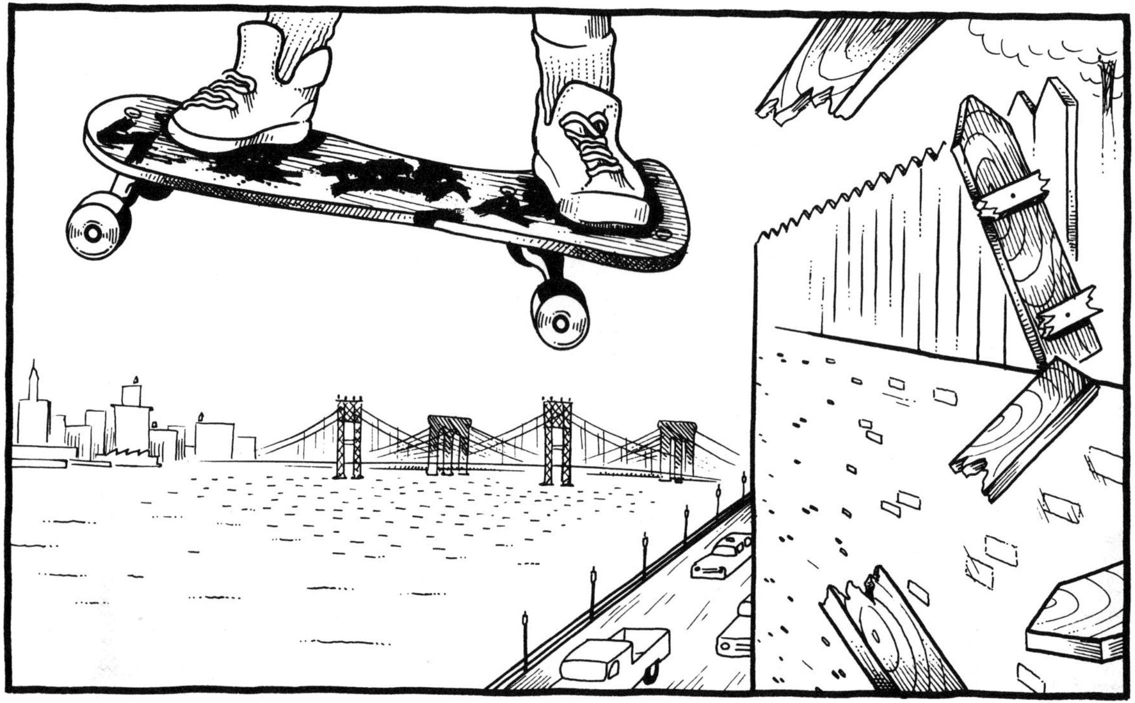

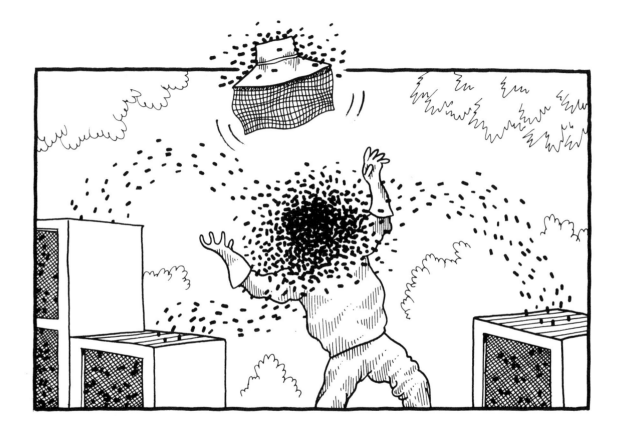

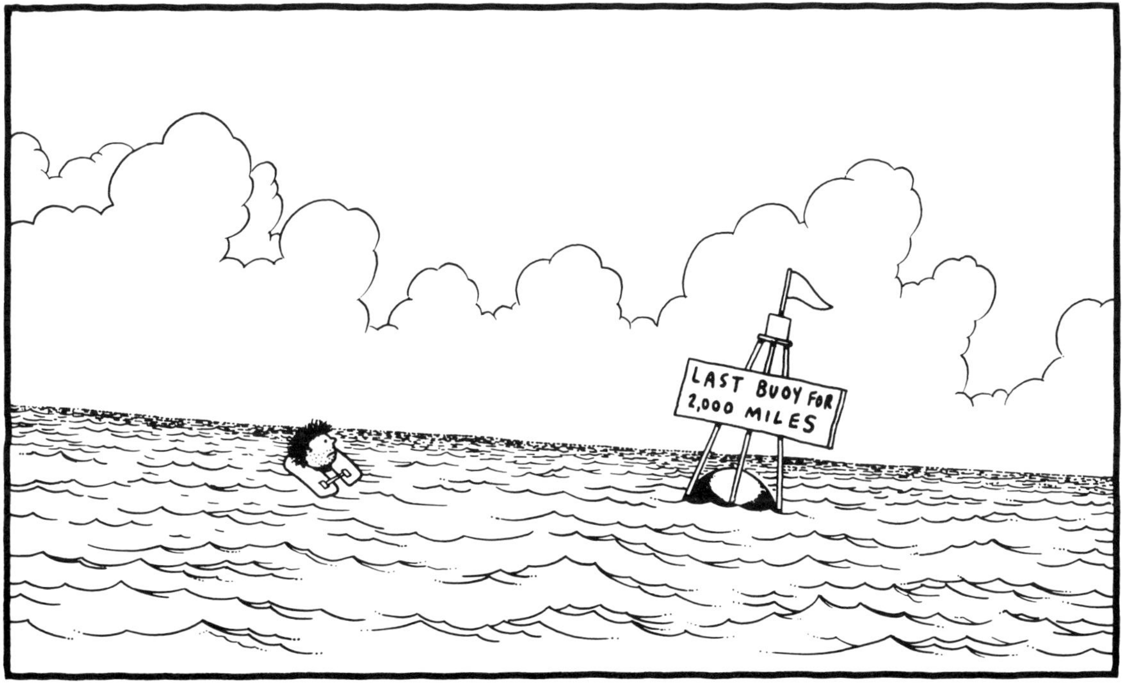
LAST BUOY FOR
2,000 MILES

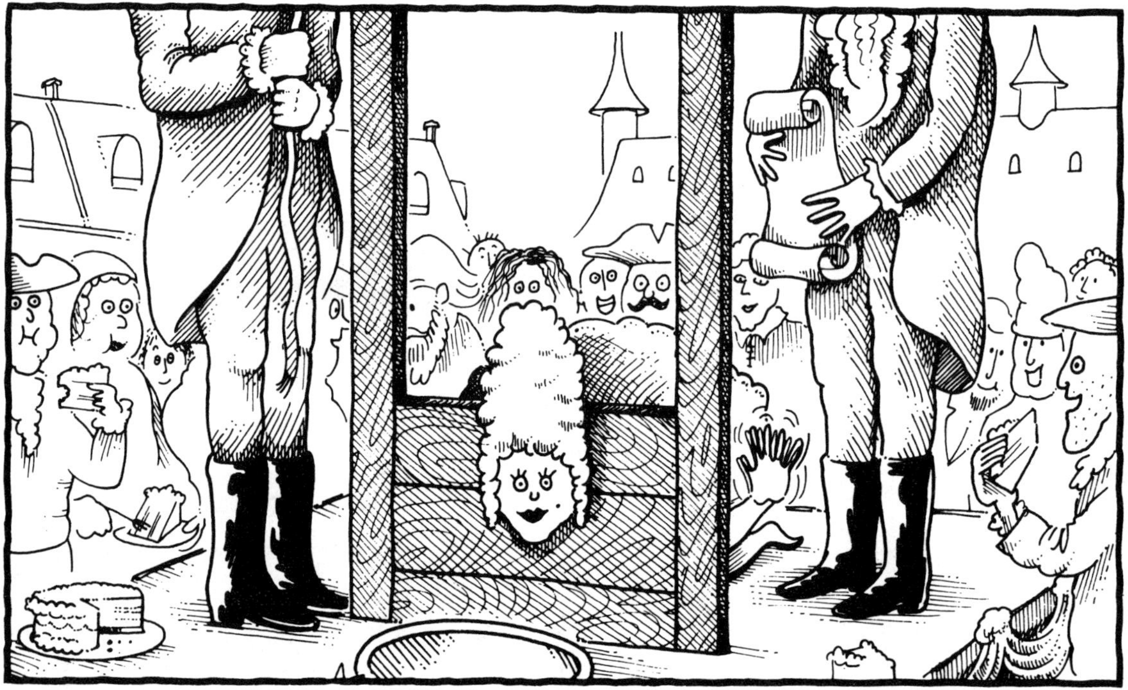

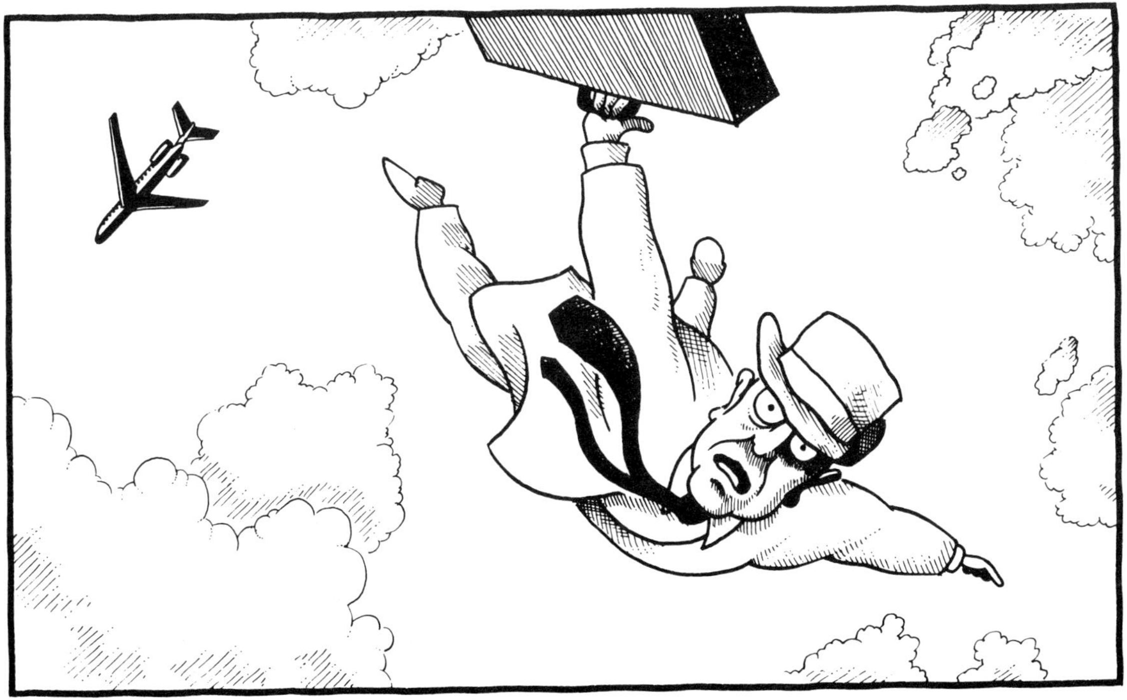

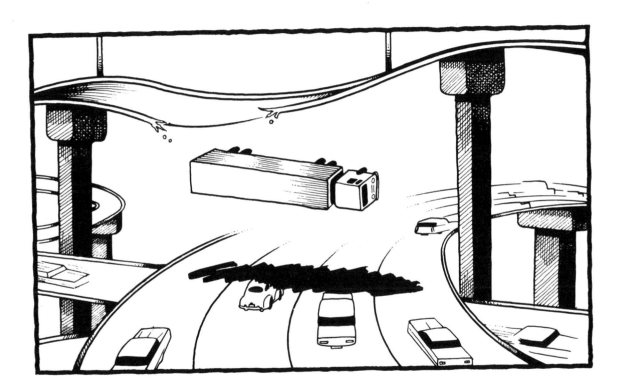

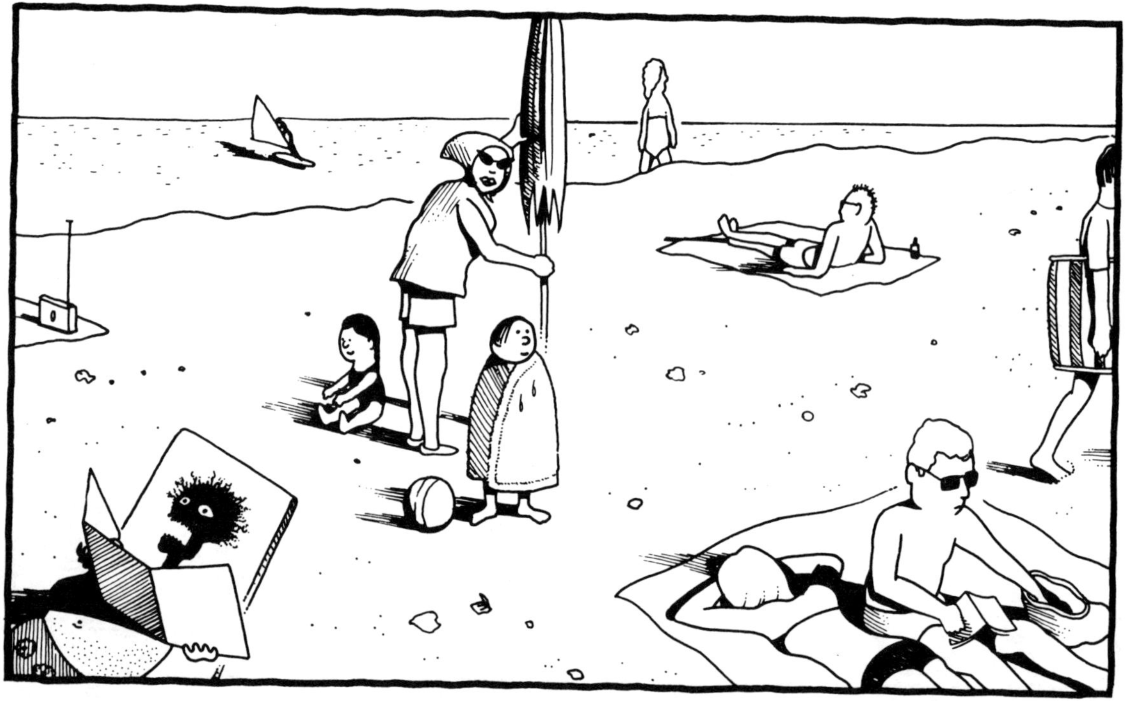

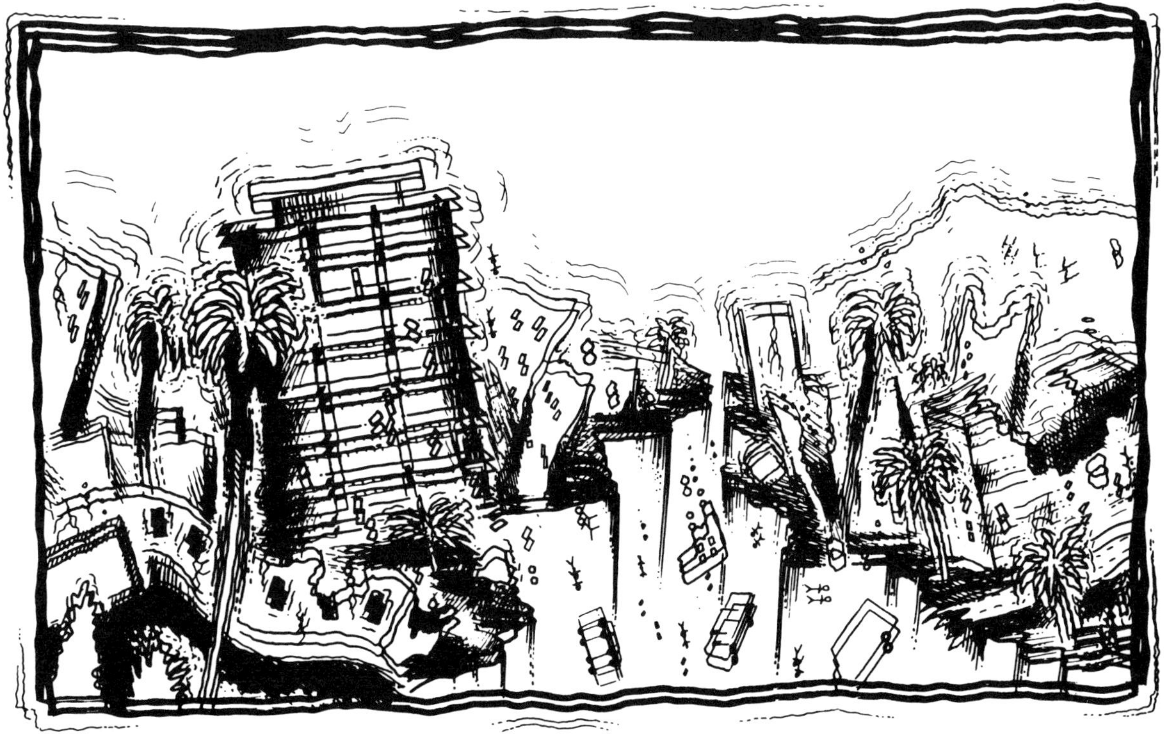

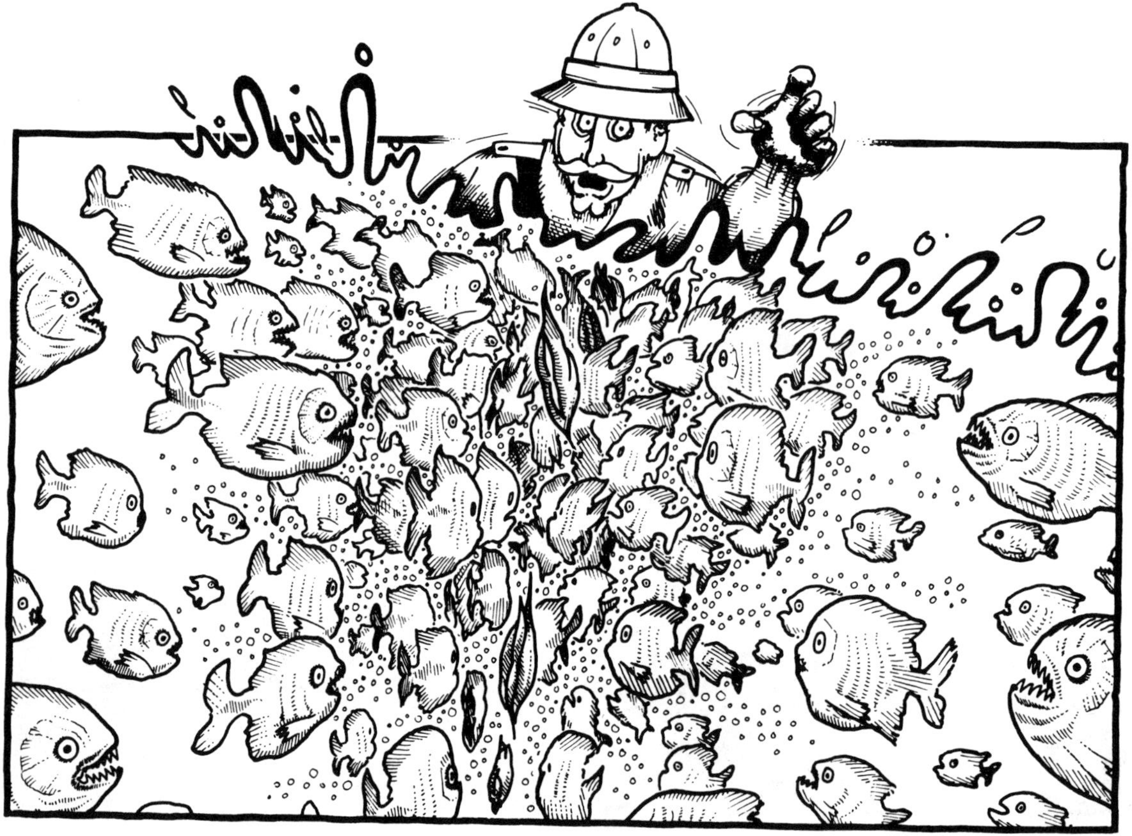

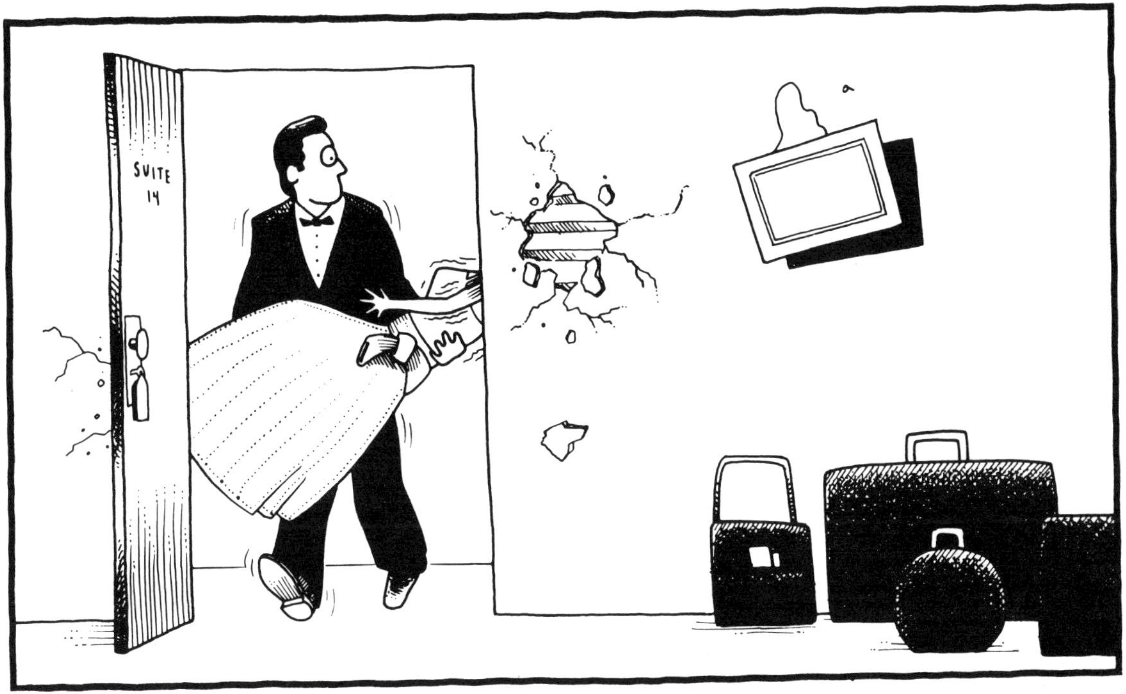
SUITE
14

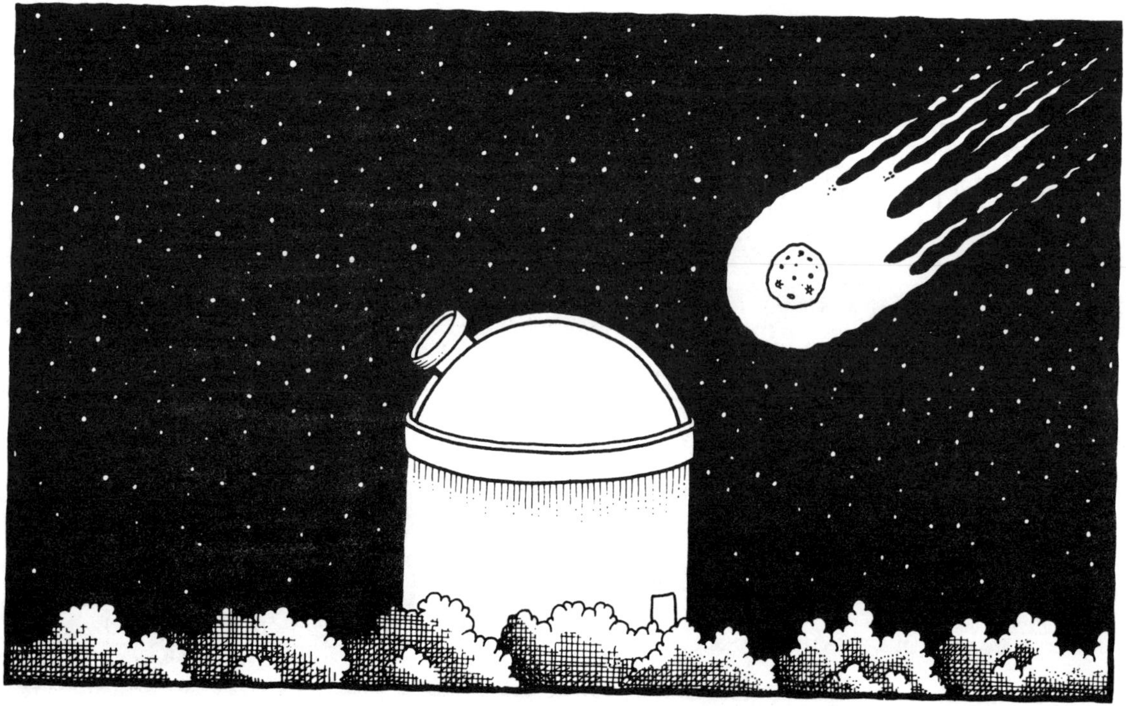

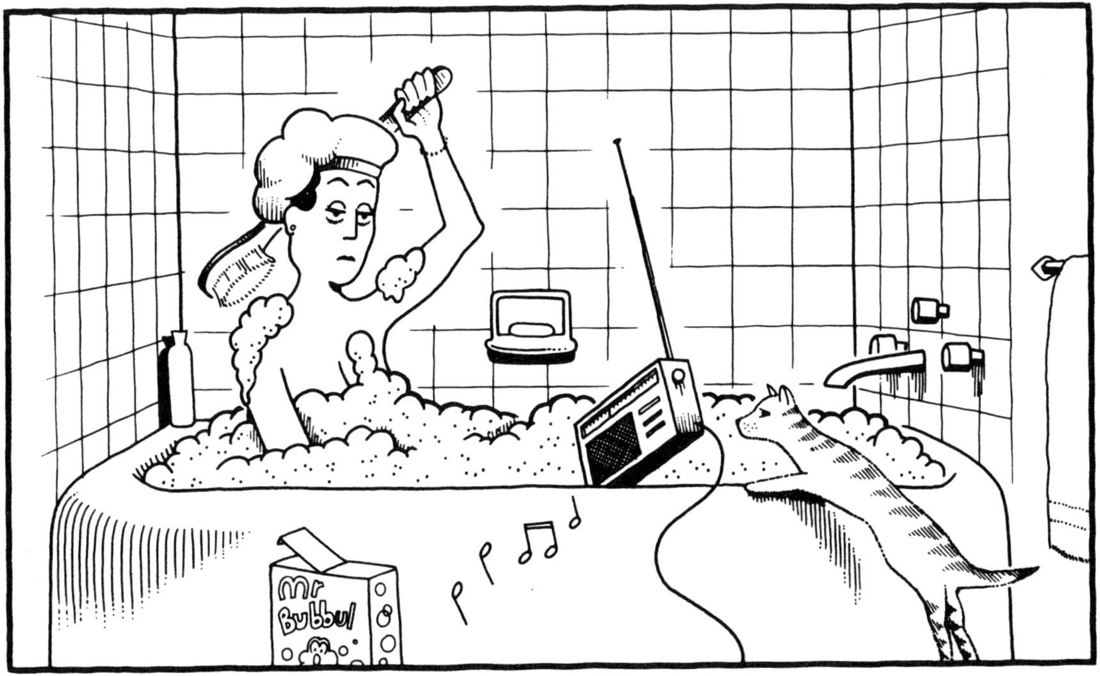
Mr
Bubbul

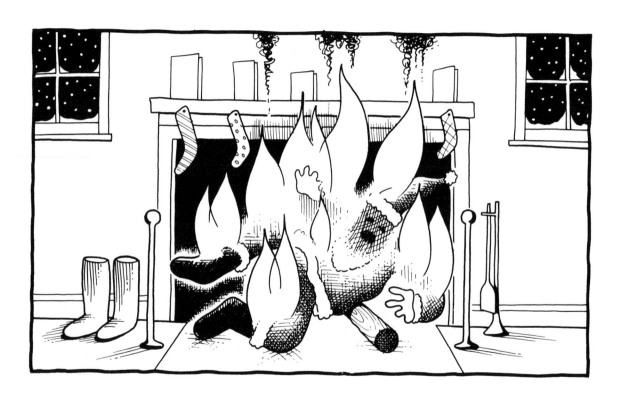

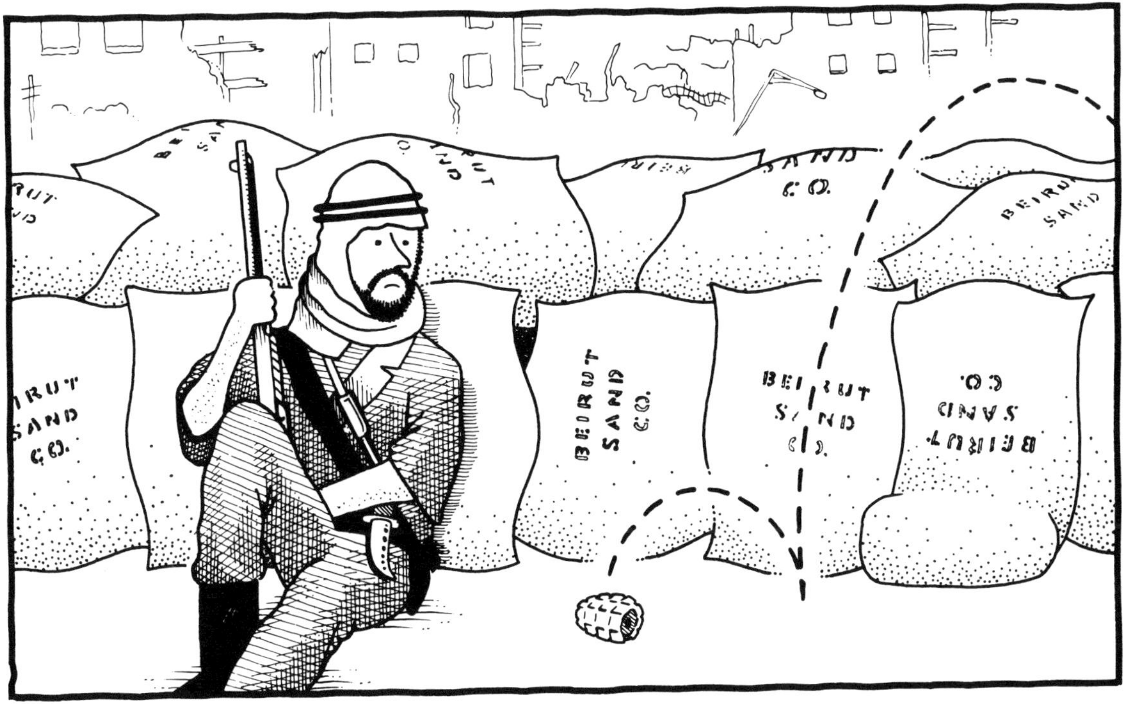
BEIRUT SAND CO.
BEIRUT SAND CO.

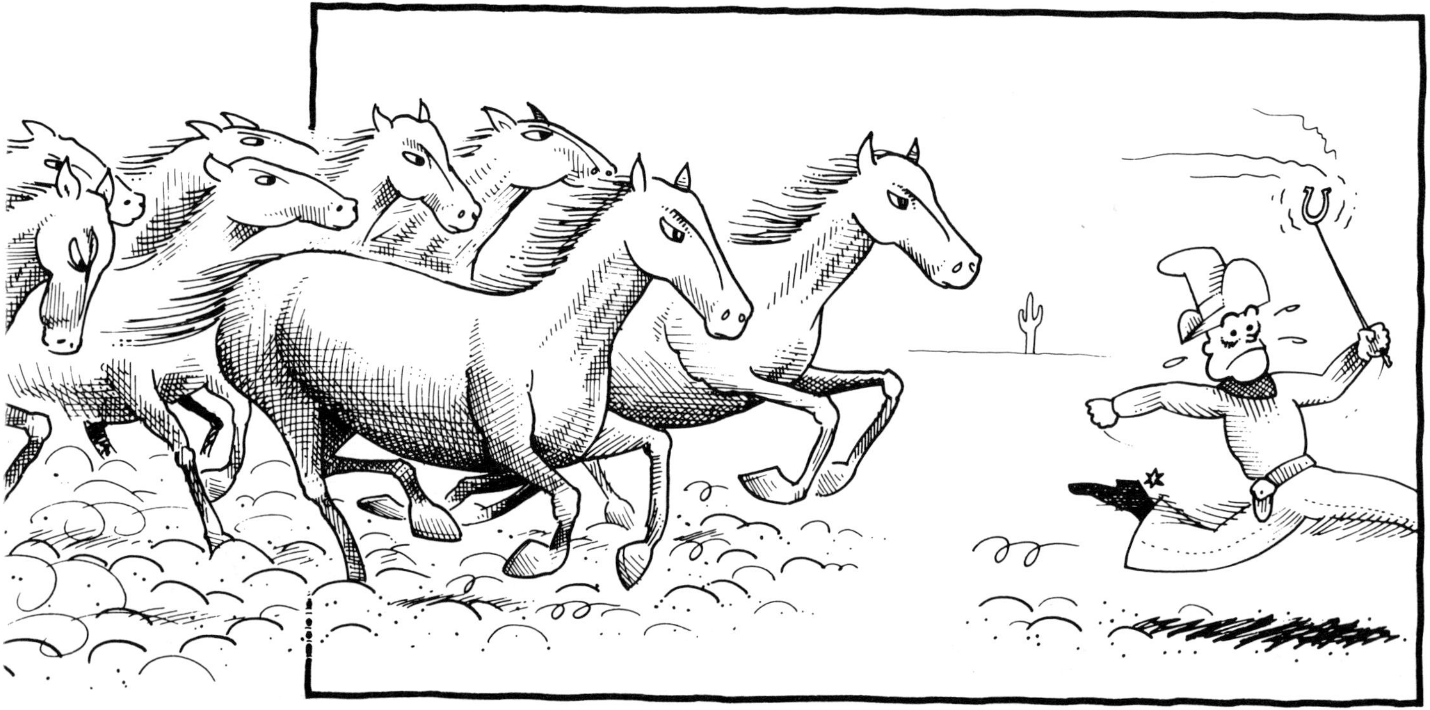

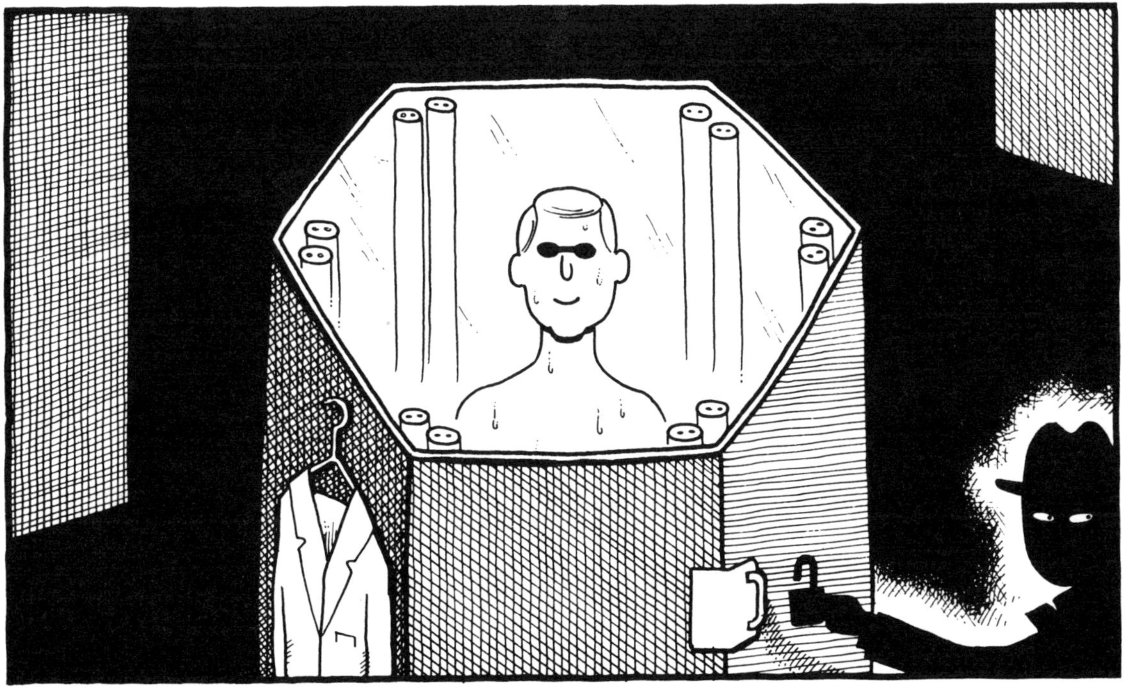

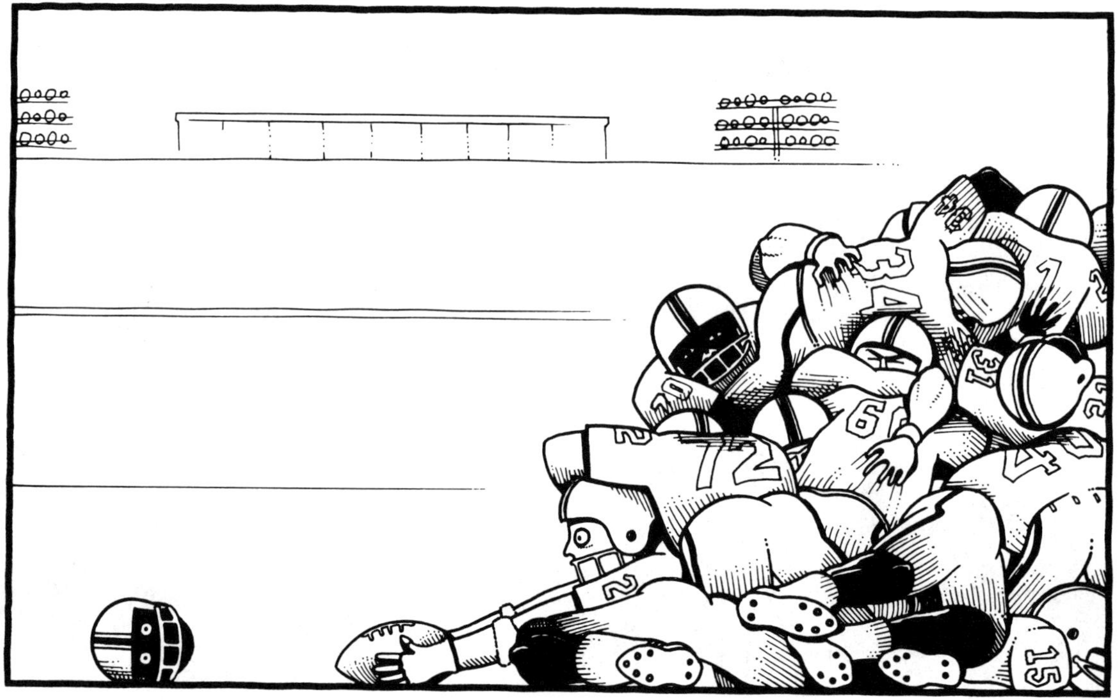

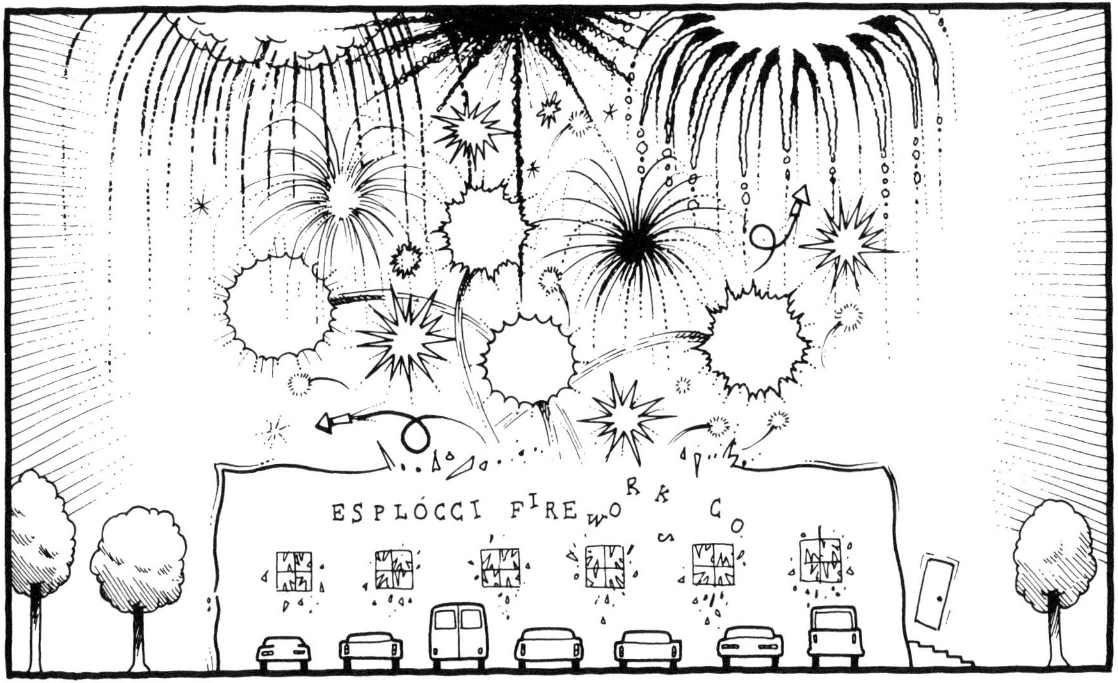
ESPLÓCCI FIREWORKS CO.

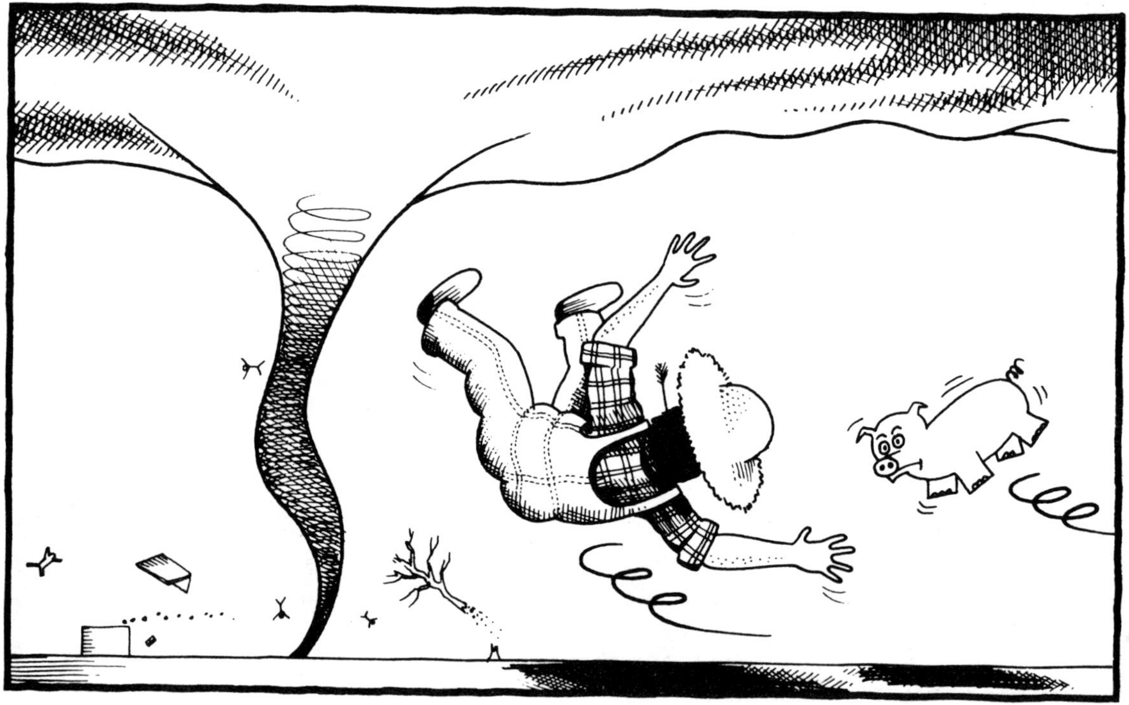

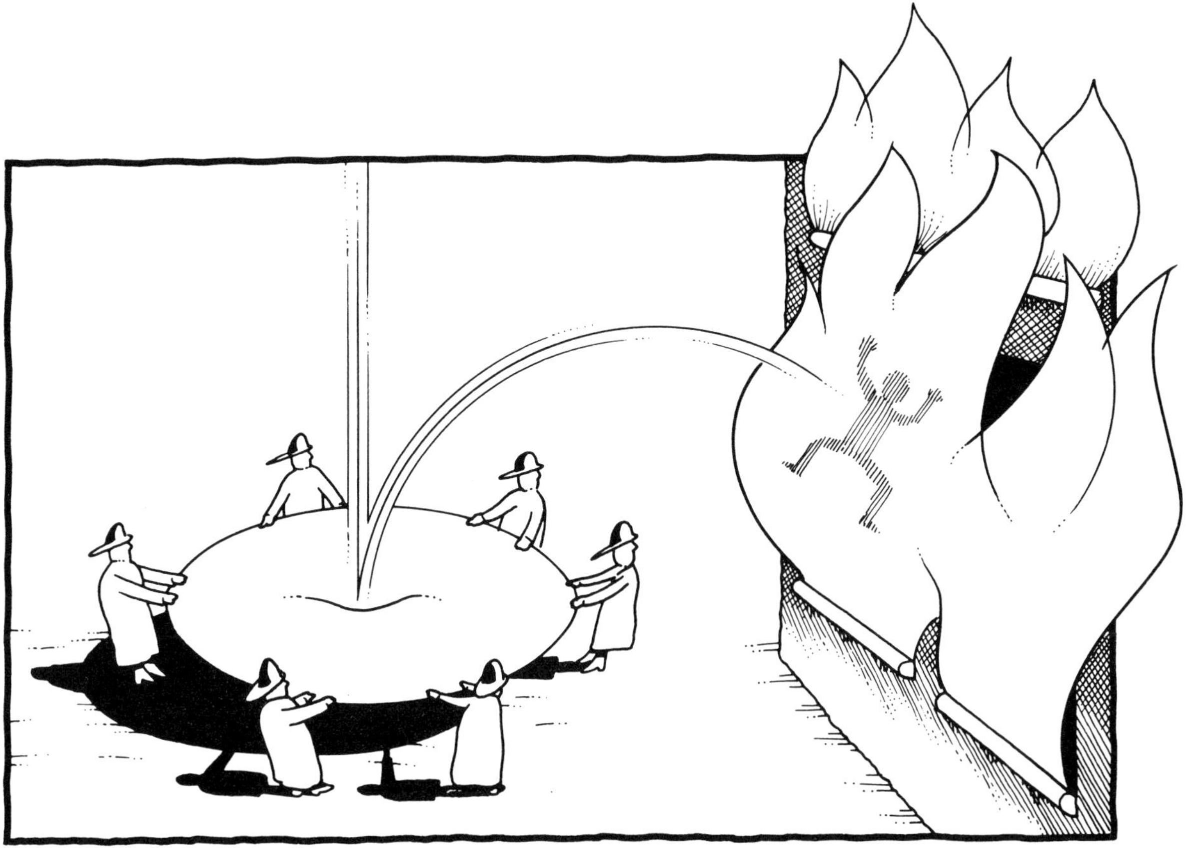

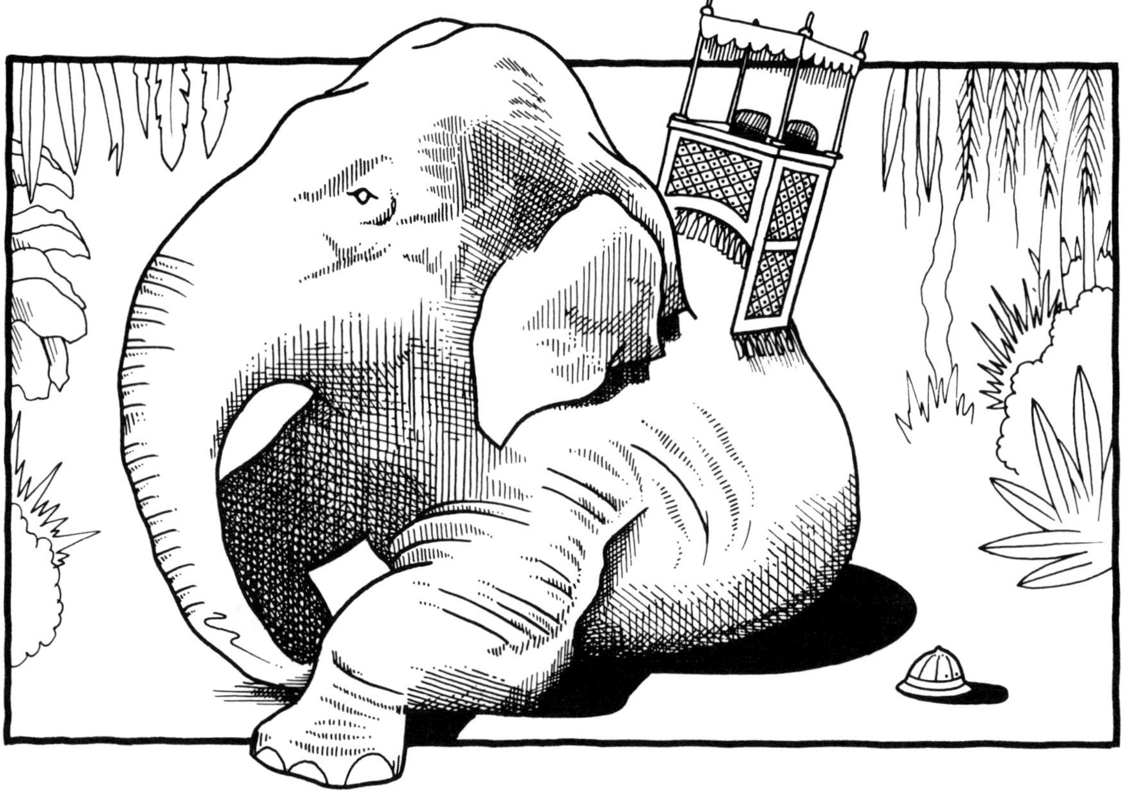

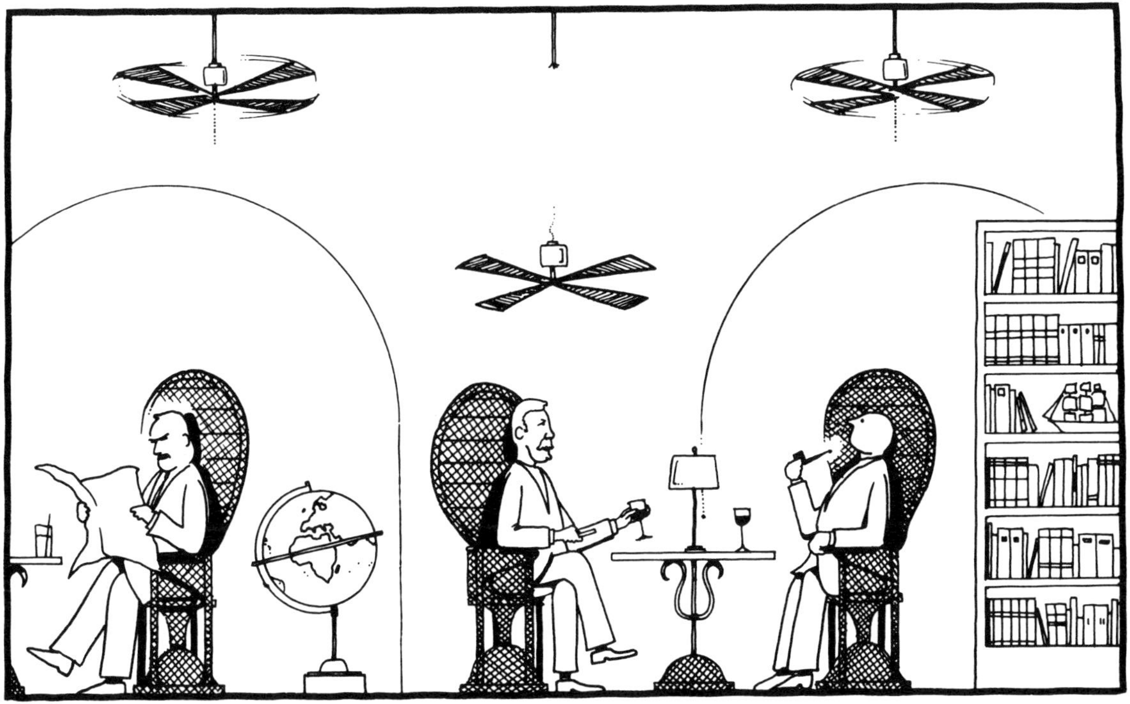

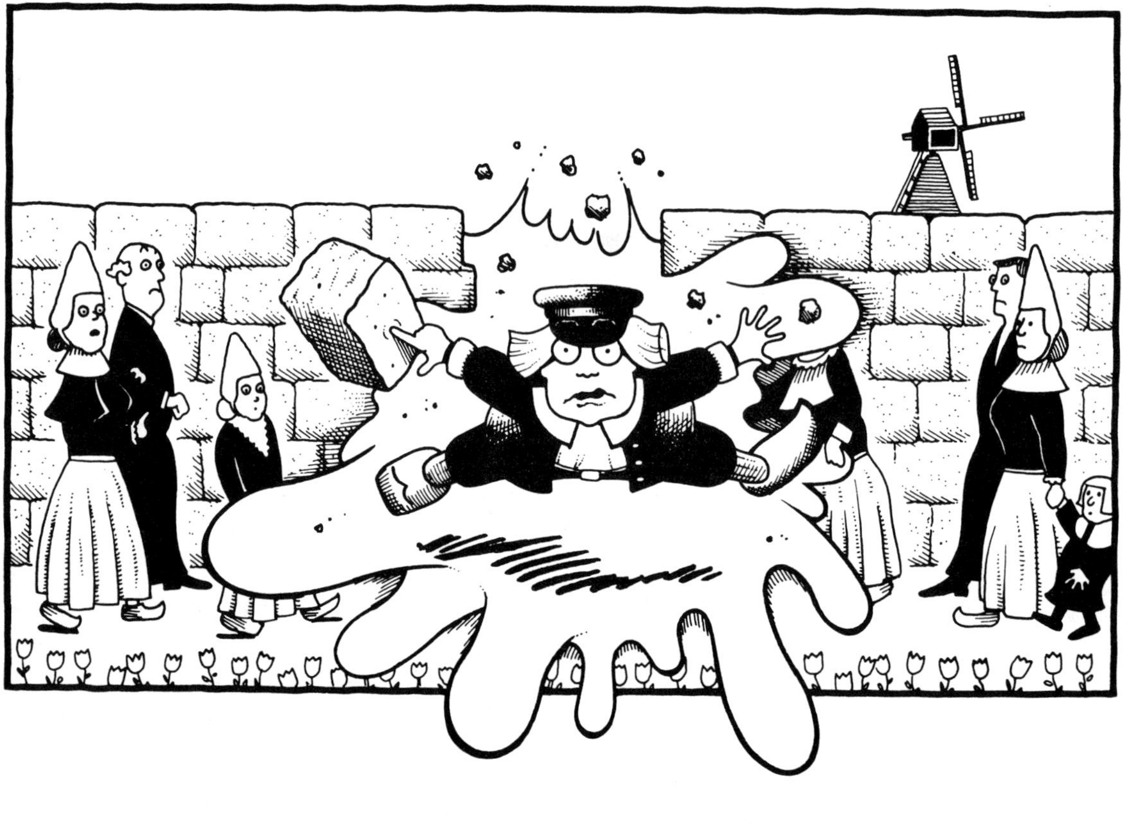

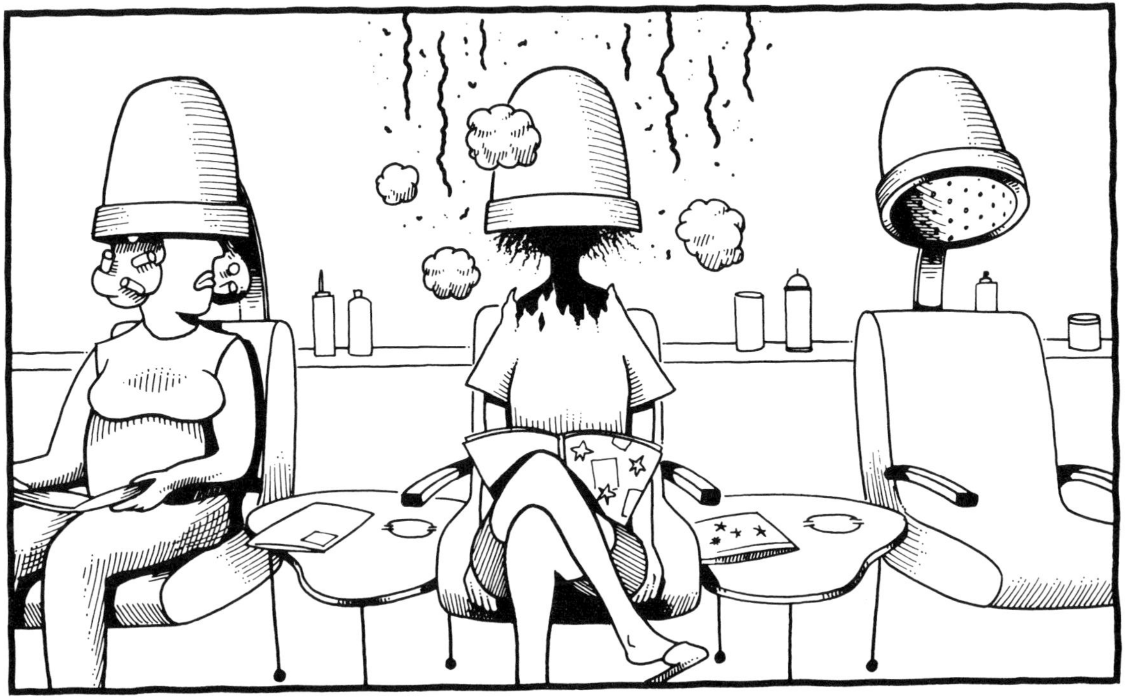

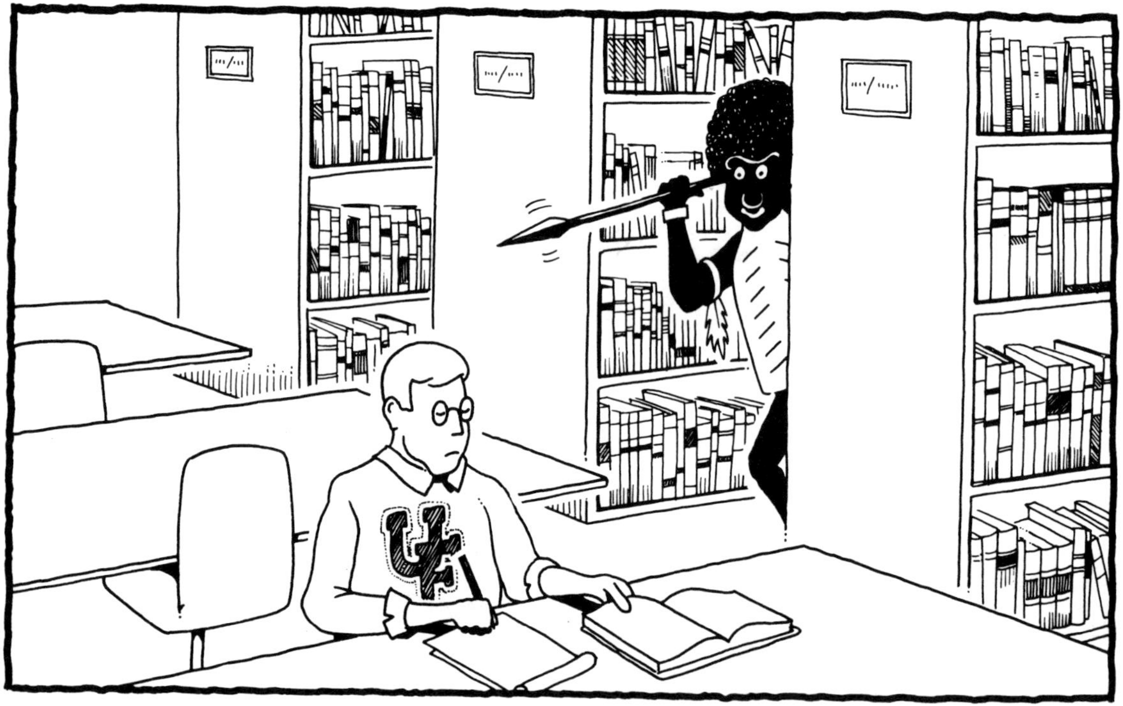

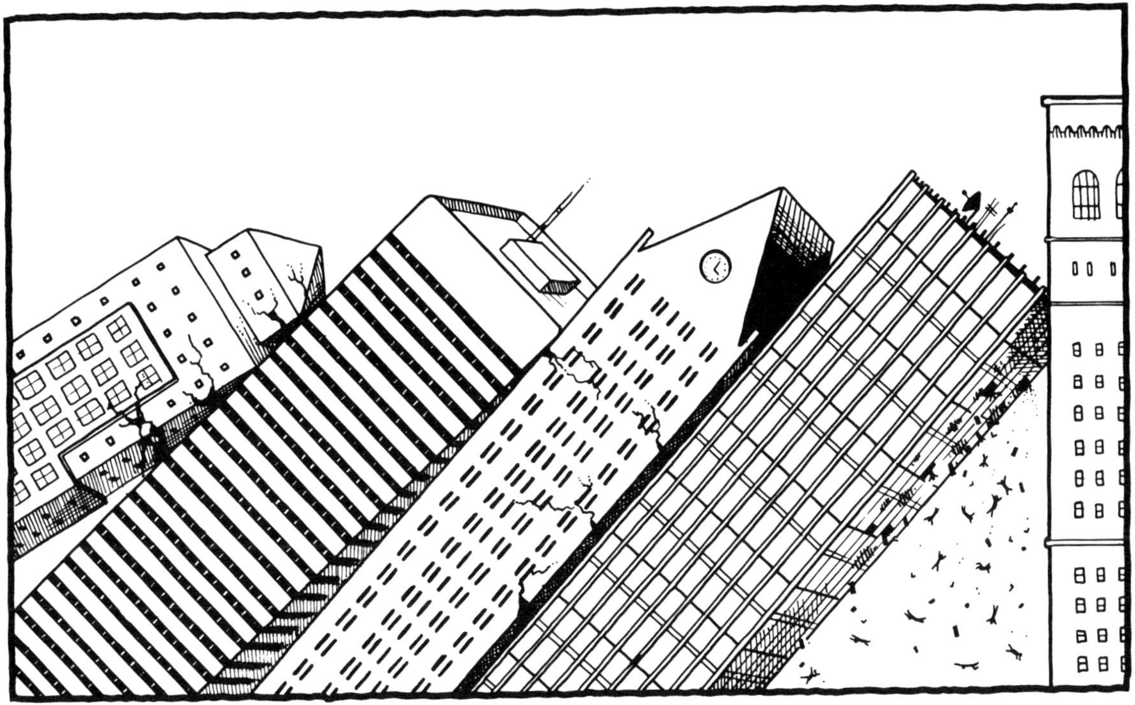

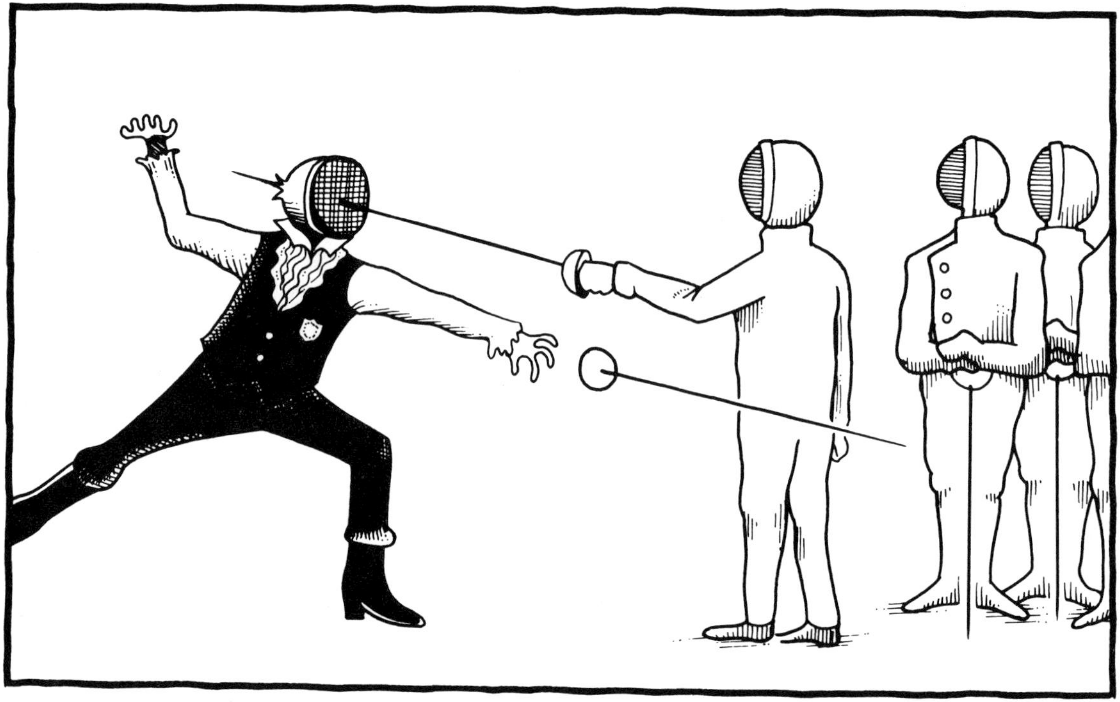

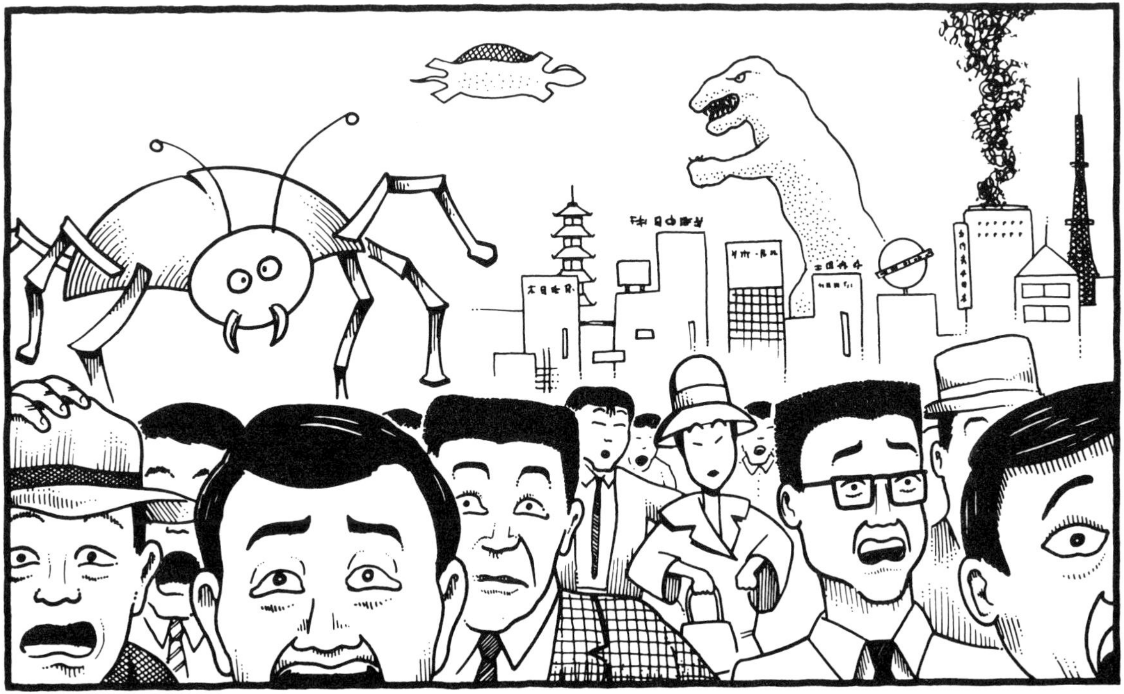

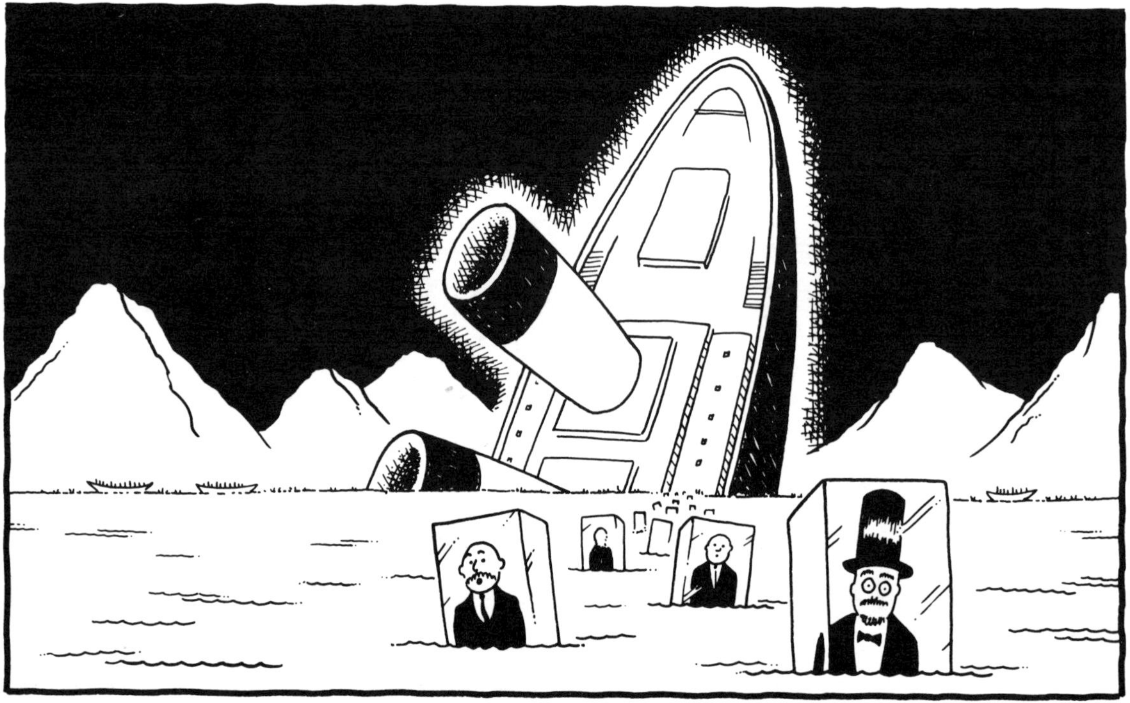

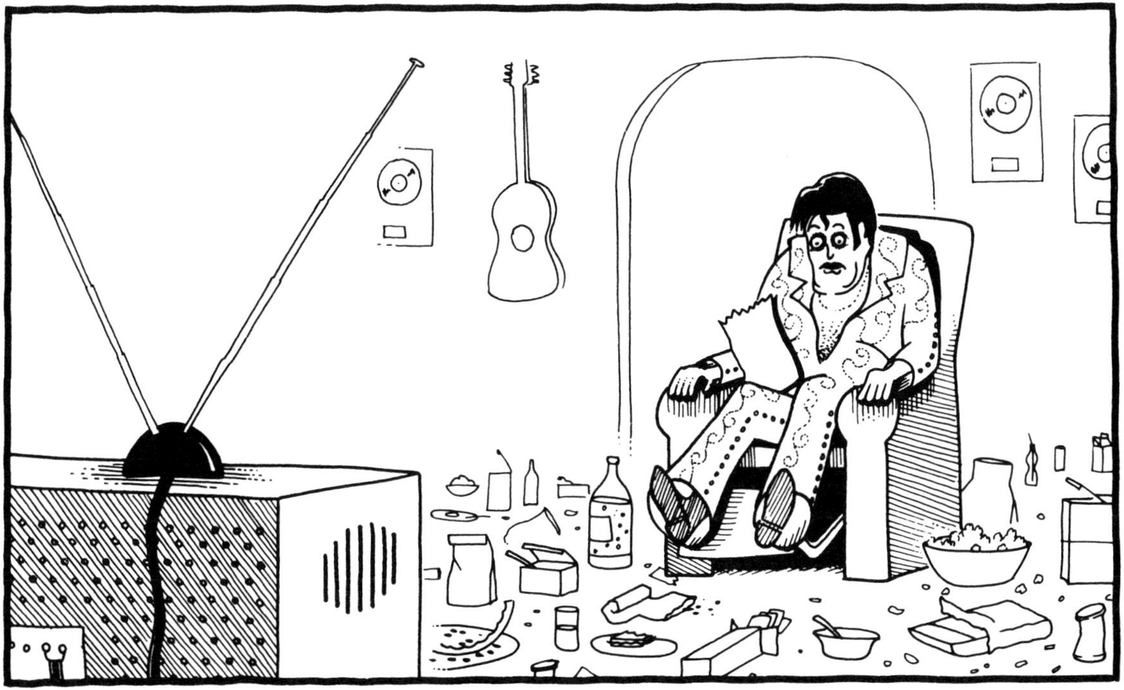

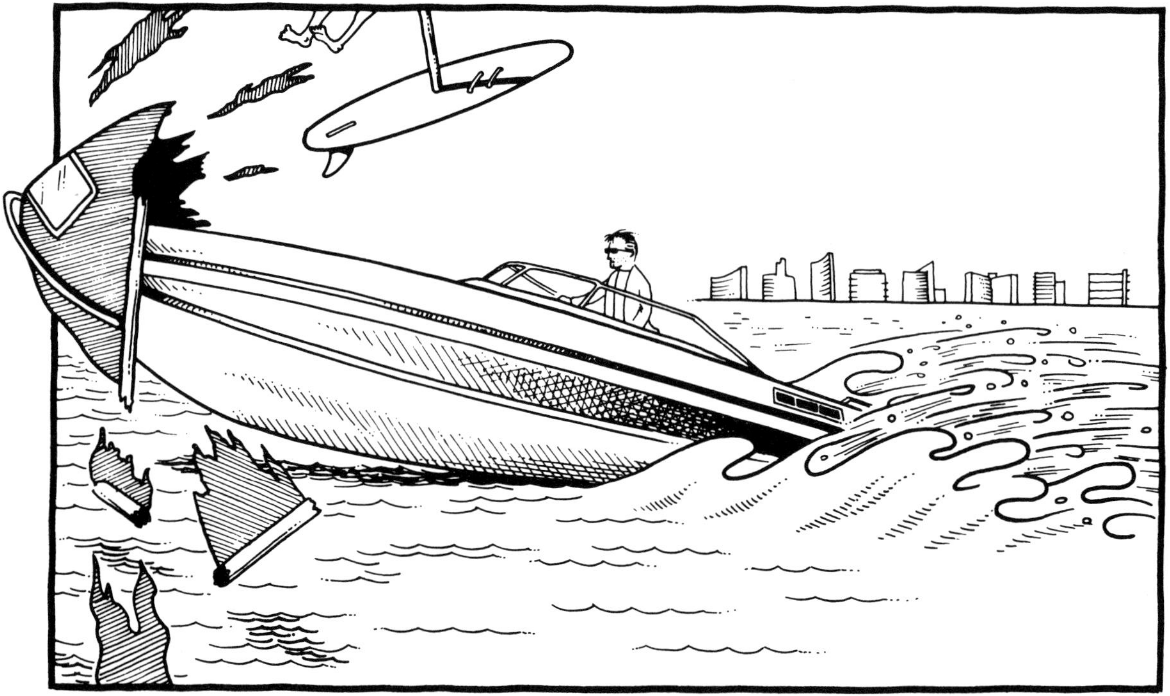

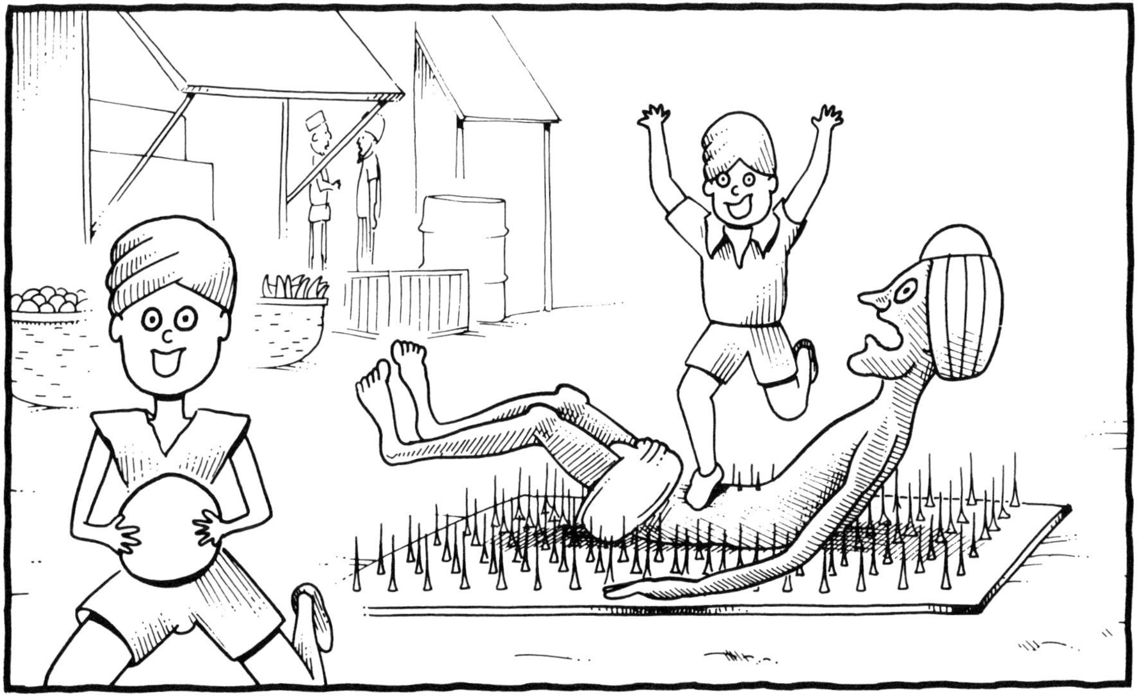

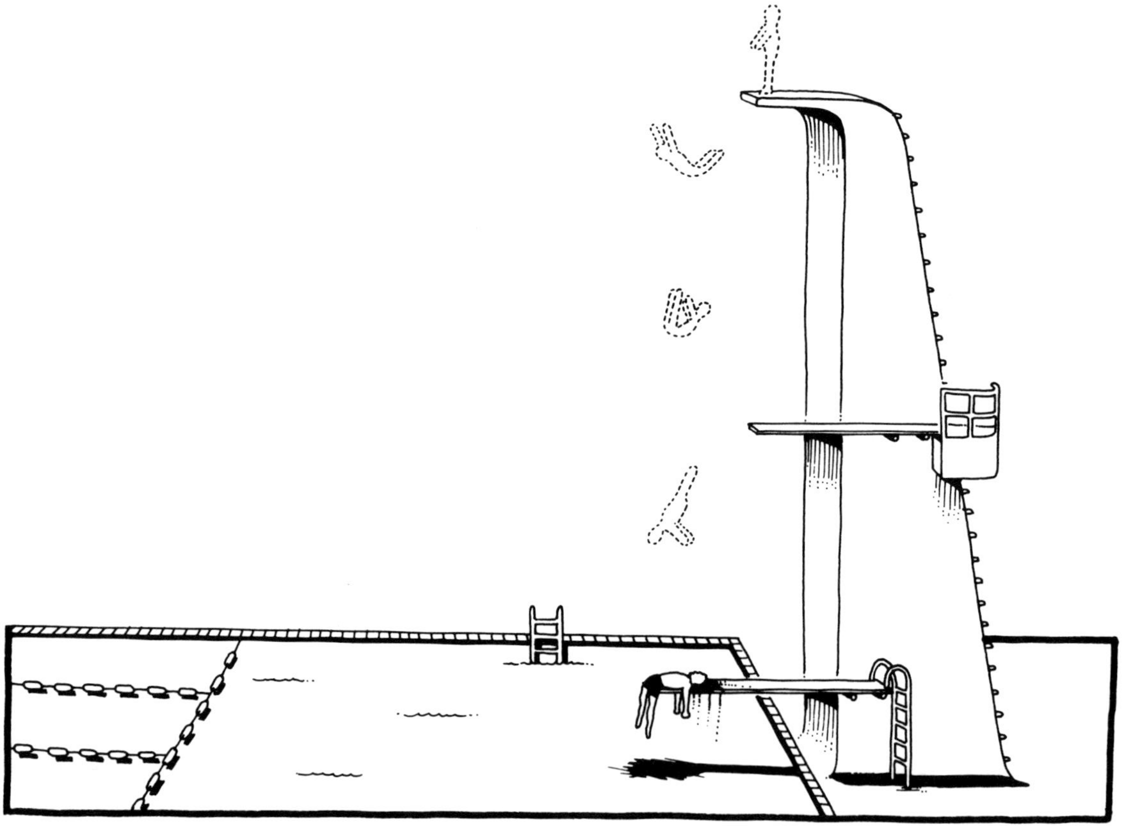

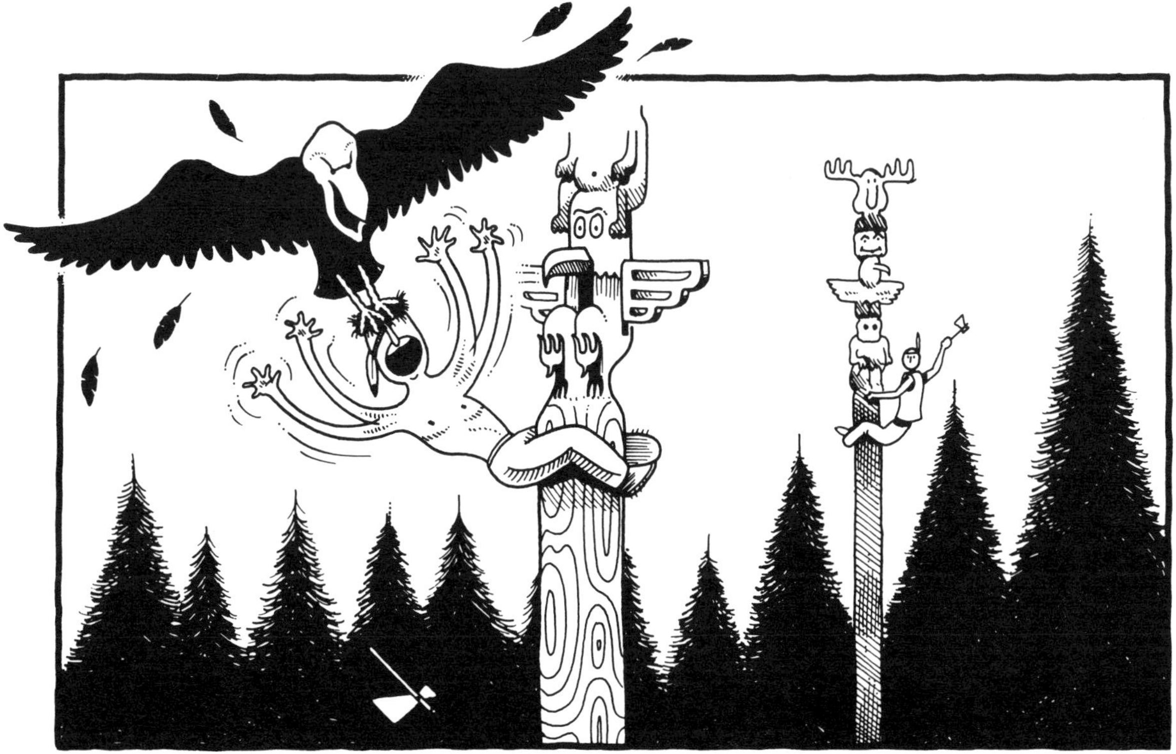

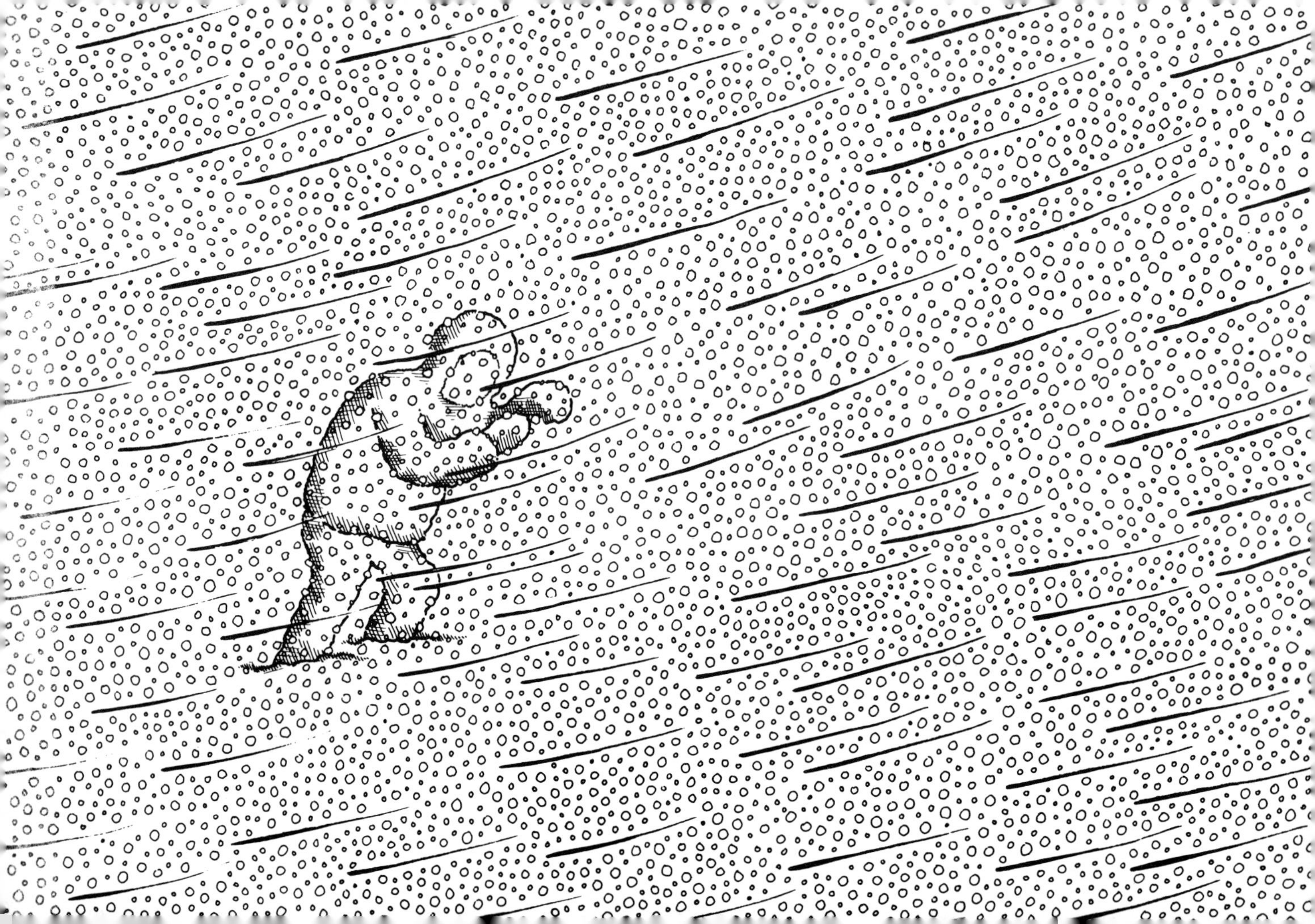

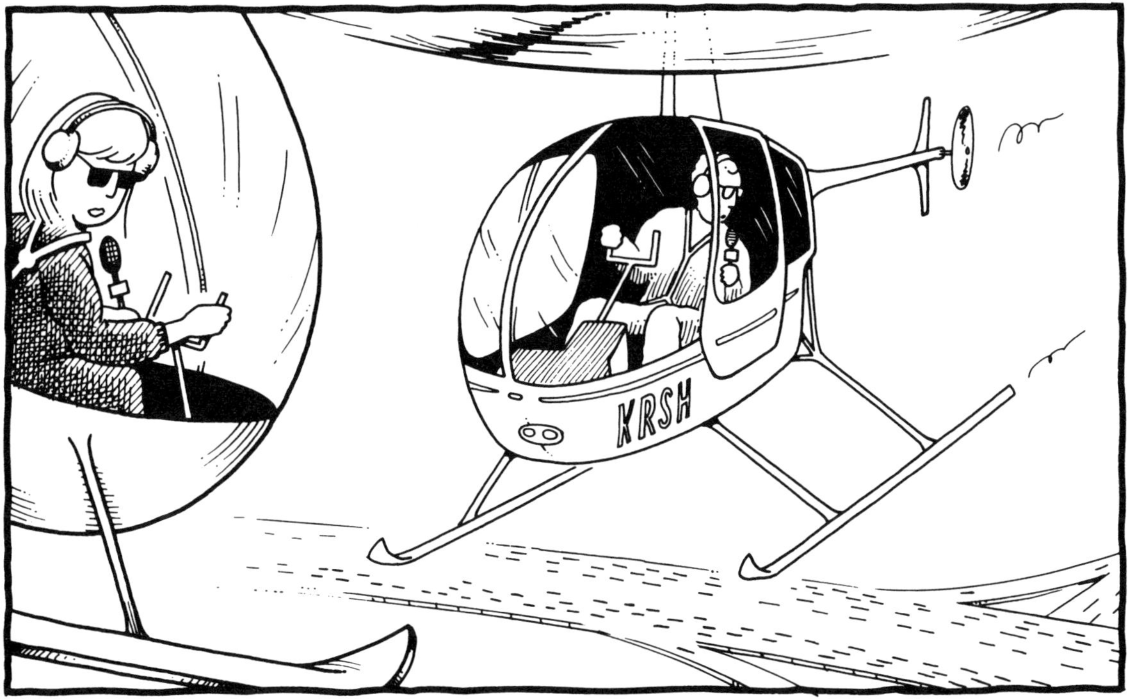
KRSH

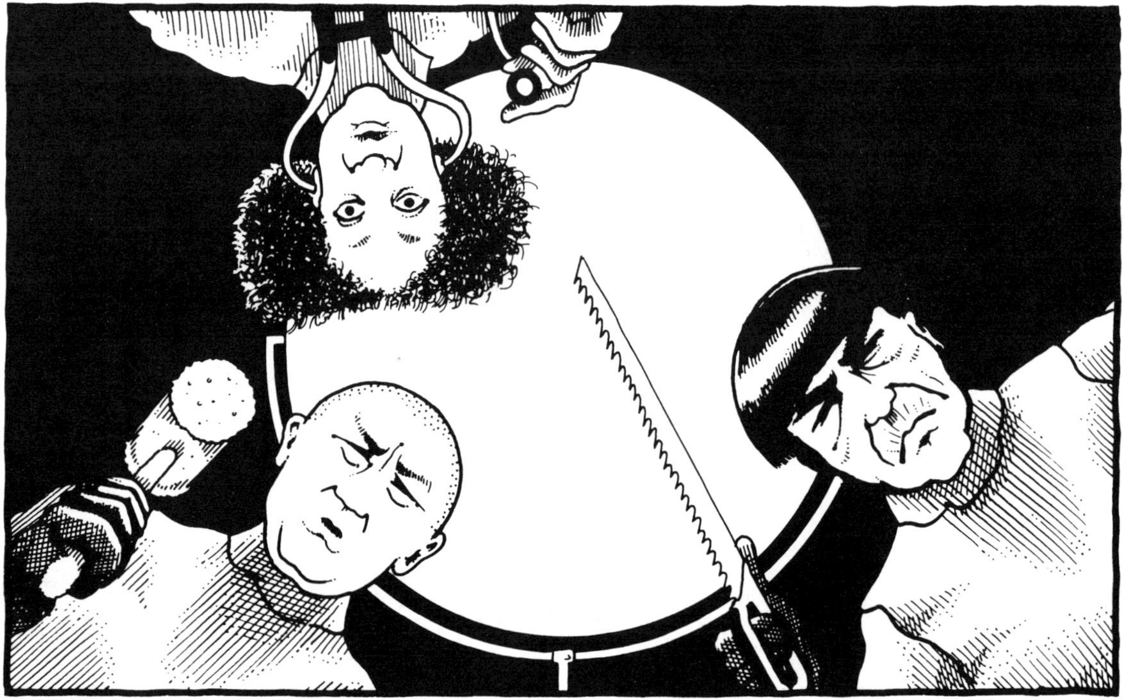

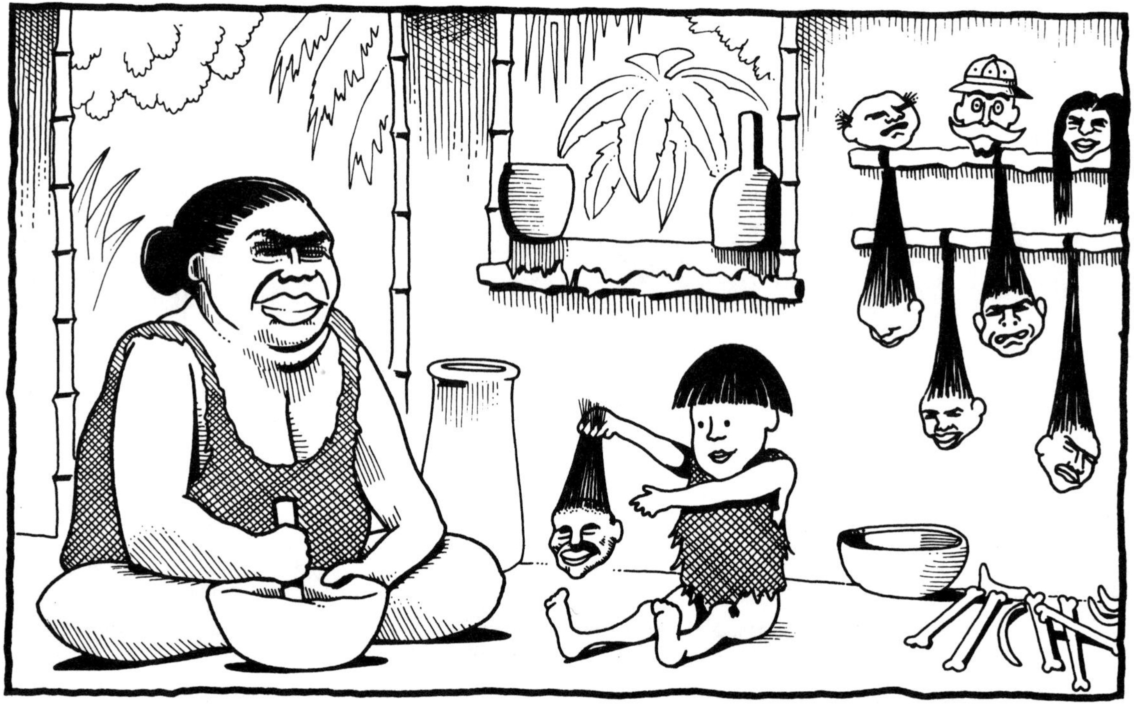

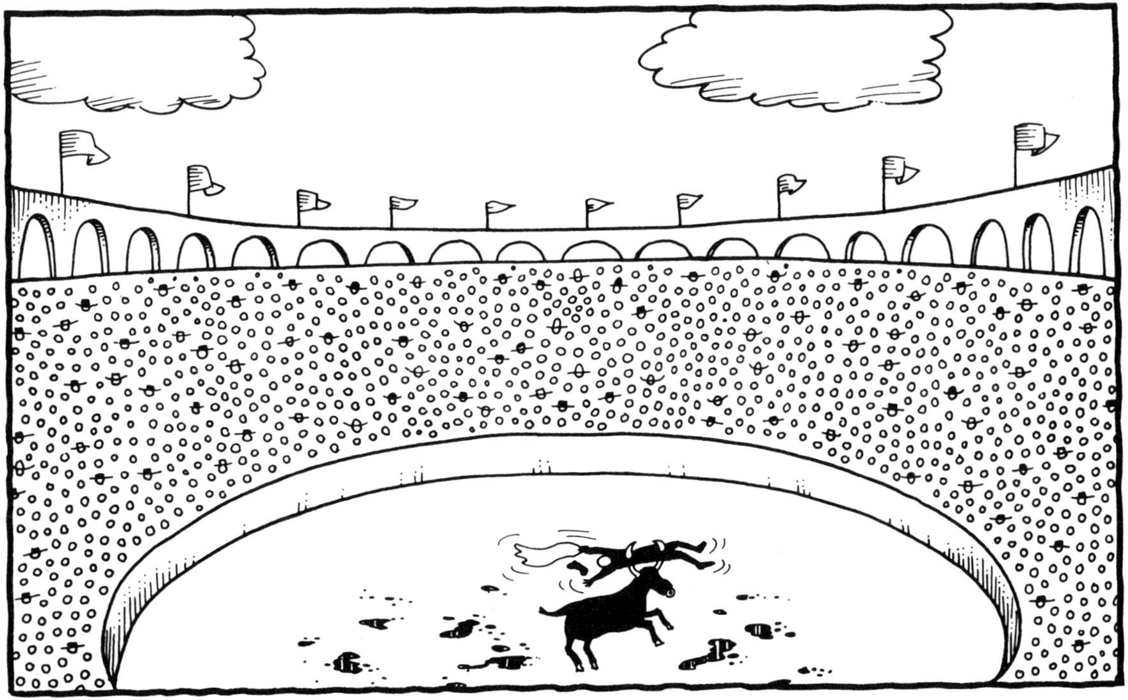

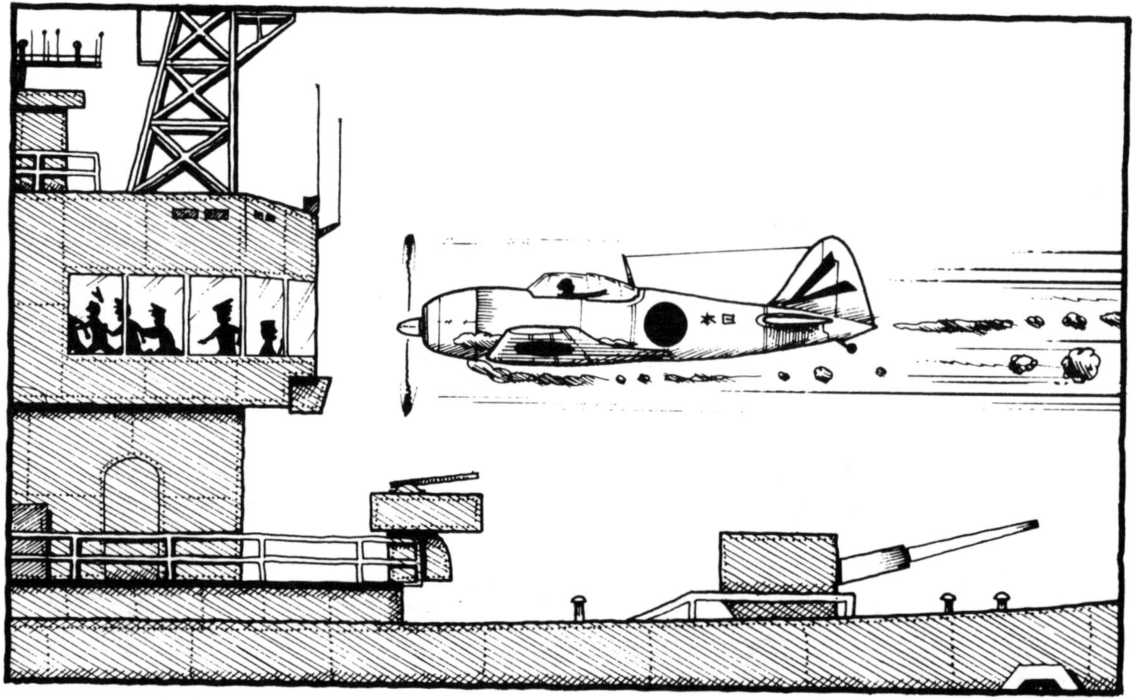

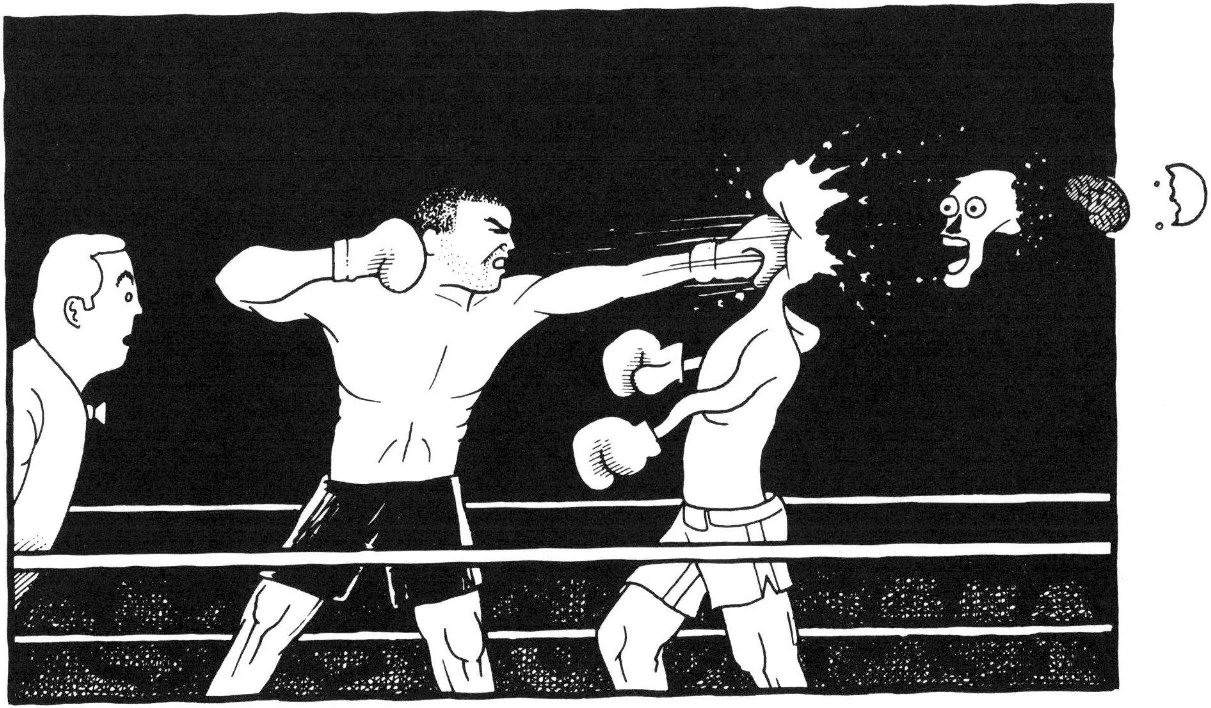

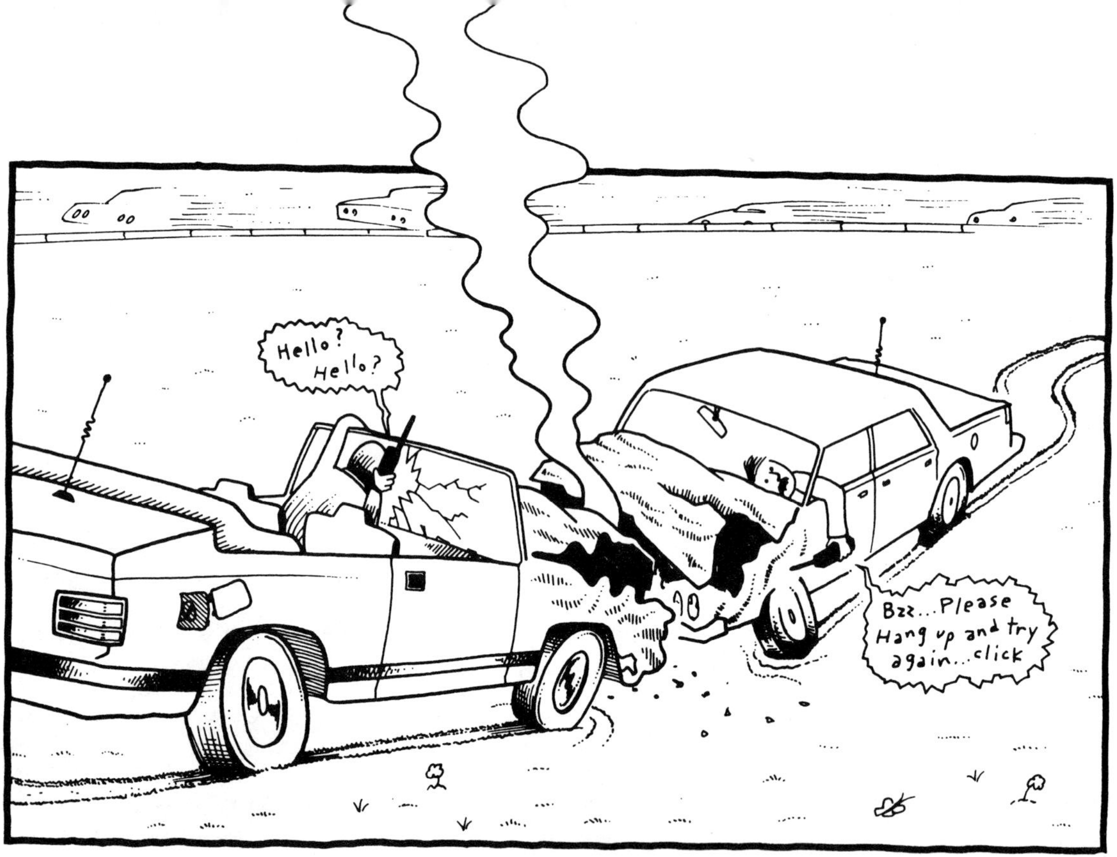
Hello? Hello?
Bzz... Please Hang up and try again... click

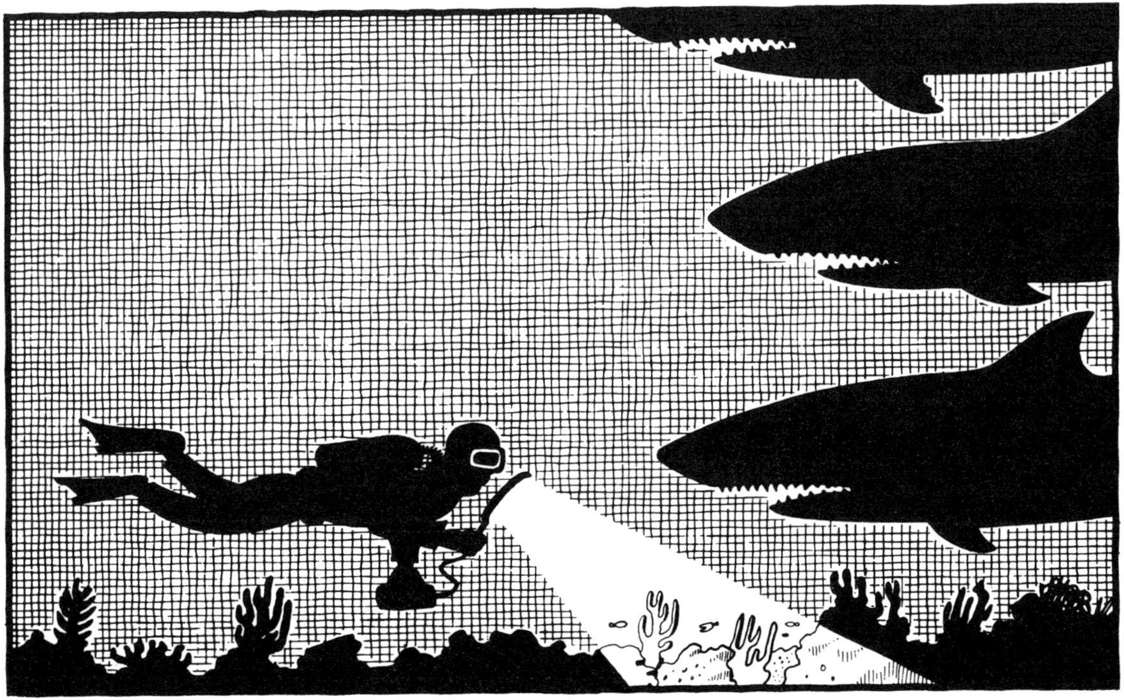

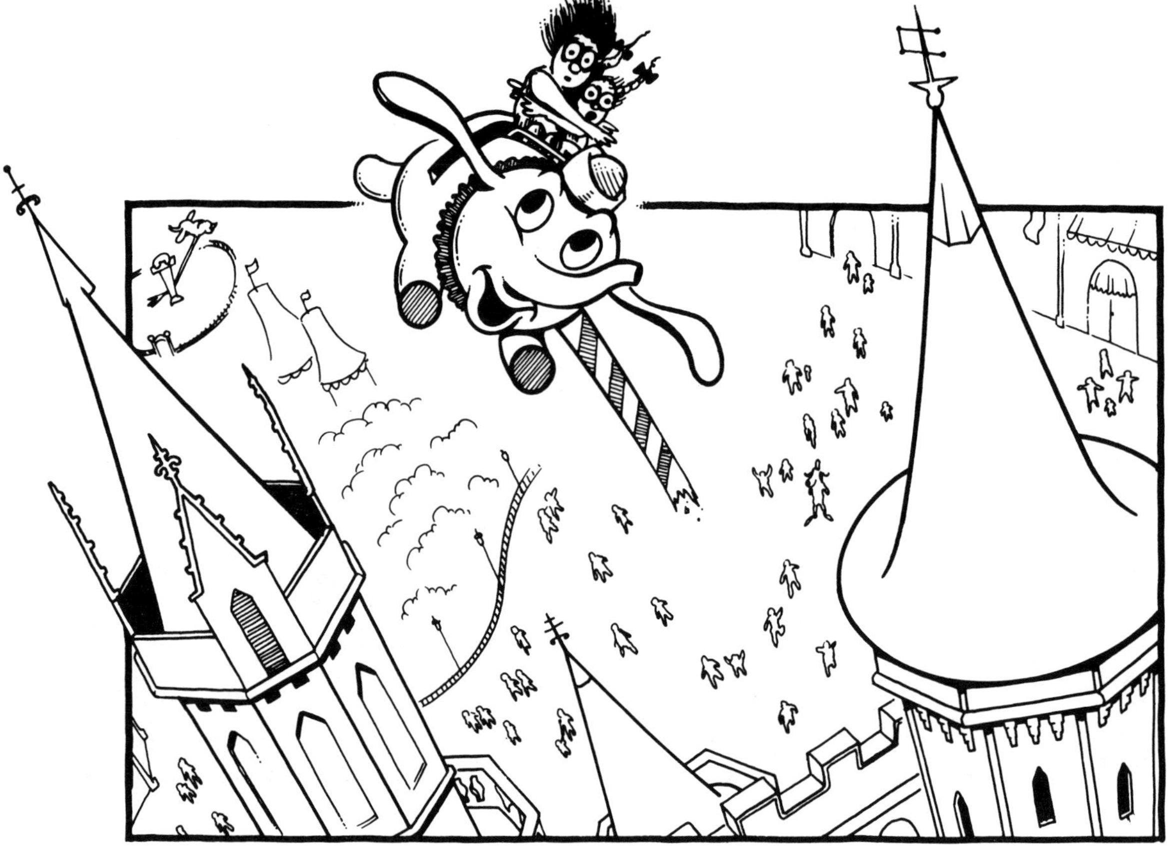

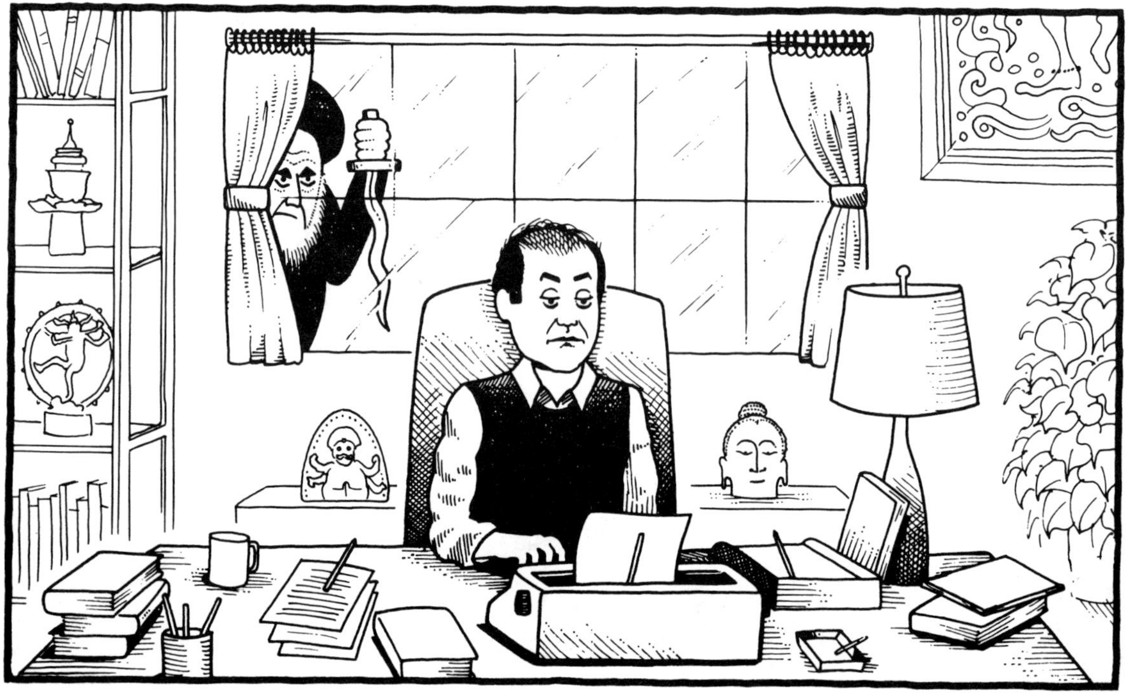

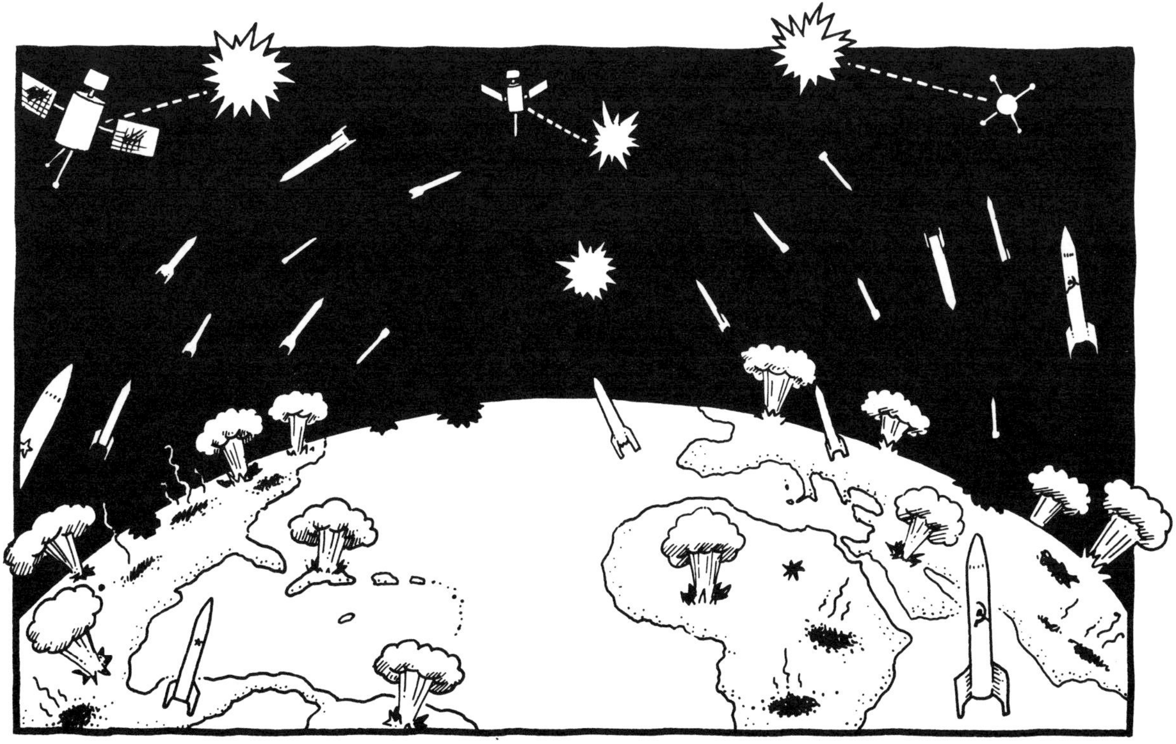